Kim

My Long Night

Printed in the United States of America

Library of Congress Catalogue Number 75-18908

ISBN 1-933641-15-0
ISBN-13 978-1-933641-15-7

Kim

My Long Night

Kim Wickes

with Hugh Steven

Kim's Ministries
P.O. Box 292
West Memphis, AR. 72303

For all who love Kim

Appreciation

I would like to thank each one who in love for God and Kim supplied important anecdotes and information.

Most especially to Kim herself, for her honesty, freshness of faith, radiance, incredible memory, and almost total recall.

And to Norma, my wife, who supports, loves, encourages, and, while still being her own person, edits and types for me!

Finally I would like to express my thanks to Jesus Christ our Lord, for whom we write.

Contents

Foreword

In my eighty-four years on planet Earth, at the writing of this item, and traveling to eighty-one nations on Bible tours and missions, I have met only a few Christians whom I felt were worthy to apply the words of Paul in Philippians 1:21 to their life and testimony: "For me to live is Christ." Kim Wickes is one of these very few God-blessed Christians.

Although a terrible tragedy took Kim's eyesight at the age of three, God blessed her with a glorious voice that has sung the wonderful story of so great salvation in her Lord Jesus Christ to millions around the world. How many souls will be in Heaven due to the testimony and songs of Kim Wickes will not be known until we all get there, but I am confident there will be many . . . more than we can count. To think what this one person has done to overcome all the challenges she has faced through faith proves the truth of Matthew 19:26, that all things are possible with God.

Paul Harvey, in one of his commentaries, remarked of Kim's faith and talents, that she has the "might and majesty of a heavenly host of angels." I introduce the reader to Kim Wickes, and trust that she will be as much of an inspiration to you as she has been to me and millions of others.

—Noah W. Hutchings

Introduction

The anthem was fine. So too was the minister's enunciation—the finest it could be. This was Southern California, and to every degree the morning worship service was a masterful production. An eight-piece orchestra complete with a brace of kettle drums accompanied the flawless performance of the well-rehearsed choir. There was even a Robert Redford–look-alike baritone with a gunfighter moustache to titillate the sophisticated audience.

If there was a hint of passivity, it was understandable, for excellent music was the norm here. (It's difficult to make your mouth water on a full stomach!) And then it happened. There was a slight commotion and shifting of chairs as a choir member led her to center stage, lowered the microphone to accommodate her four-foot-nine-inch stature, then turned and left her alone. Her blindness was evident, yet the bulletin gave no hint of what was to come. It simply said, "ALLELUJAH—MOZART—Kim Wickes, Soprano."

Dressed in a full-length Christmas-green velvet gown and with her tiny hands folded demurely above her waist, Kim waited for the organ introduction. She had been up since 6:00 a.m., had sung at two previous services, and had given a TV performance. Yet her light yellow-brown Korean face shone with the freshness of morning dew.

As the first sonorous sounds of the organ filled the sanctuary, every eye fixed on the doll-sized performer. Tilting back her head slightly, 27–year–old Jeanie Kim Wickes opened her mouth and began to sing.

The transformation was immediate. With a single passage, the tiny, helpless-looking, eighty-five-pound figure was in total command of herself and the audience.

As I listened that Sunday morning, I wanted to describe the power, range, control, and superb technical training with all the superlatives I knew. I settled for a single word—electric!

Her close friend Cliff Barrows used the same word when he described Kim's impact on an international congress in Lausanne, Switzerland, where she was given a standing ovation. "When the camera projected Kim onto that huge screen at the conference," said Cliff, "the impact was electric!"

The congregation didn't stand that first Sunday morning I heard Kim sing. Protocol demanded a tighter control of emotions. But nothing could constrain them from clapping. Immediately after Kim's final full-bodied Allelujah ended, the congregation applauded. Some were timid at first and hesitated. But as the impact of what they had just heard sunk into their minds, each one expressed audibly what was in their hearts.

As the writer who was soon to walk deeper into her life, I felt that her music came from another dimension—a dimension that clashed against reality. Elizabeth Mannion, her voice teacher at Indiana University, said, "Kim's music brings out the best in everyone."

It's true. When Kim sings she brings into focus the high excitement and exhilarating joy of life.

This is the true story of Kim, who though physically blind sees more than most sighted people. It's the story of true grit, determination, courage—both hers and that of her adoptive parents, George and Eva Wickes. It's the story of a girl who by her own admission believes that her blindness is a gift from God, and who because of her personal faith in Jesus Christ has turned a so-called handicap to her own advantage and to the timeless glory of God.

—Hugh Steven

1. A Day for Dreams

How could I tell them that kissing felt yucky? I couldn't speak English, and these two people—my new American parents—couldn't speak Korean. Besides being blind, I was frightened! I felt sick to my stomach and tired from flying twenty-eight hours from Seoul, Korea, to Portland, Oregon.

And why were they calling me Jeanie when my real name was Kim Eun Joon—kissing me and hugging me? The wet on my cheek was dirty and I wiped away their kisses.

For ten-year-old Kim, the affectionate kisses of her new American parents were as unexpected as an electric jolt. Legally she was now the adopted daughter of George and Eva Wickes of Dayton, Indiana. Yet as Kim stepped off that Northwest Orient turboprop aircraft on Thanksgiving Day in 1957, she was the daughter of another tradition—a tradition and way of life that considered a Western demonstration of affection intolerable.

Out of their excitement to welcome Kim and assure her of their love, George and Eva, and later their own four children, clashed head-on into fifteen centuries of Confucian ethic—an ethic which demanded strict separation of male and female children after age seven. And for Kim, whose only dim memory of affection was the occasional stroking of her shiny black hair by her Korean father, the

Wickes' caresses were the first of many frustrating adjustments into American culture and life.

Kim's first and immediate frustration was communication: she spoke almost no English. The fact was devastating. Within the space of a few hours, Kim changed from an outgoing, vivacious, energetic ten-year-old to a frightened, silent, almost-sullen child who thought the word "Indiana" on her armband meant "Indian"—the red king with feathers and spears!

Knowing only that she was now in America, Kim waited in bewildering silence to be taken to her new home. With her limited understanding of American culture, Kim thought Americans were tall and wide—that they took up too much room and made everything too big. Later, when she opened her first box of toothpaste, she knew the allegations were true. The box was larger than the tube! Even a baby's cry sounded bigger to her in America than it had in Korea.

Puzzled by Kim's reaction to their affection, George and Eva thoughtfully led a melancholy, confused Kim onto a train to begin their journey back to Dayton.

I got on this thing and sat down. At first I thought the train compartment was my new home. Then because I heard about American skyscrapers swaying in the wind, I thought that's where I was. It was only when we had to go between two cars to reach the dining car that I understood I was on a train. And then I began to remember.

Once, a long time before, when my Korean father and I were refugees trying to escape the air bombing, we wanted to get on a train. But too many others also tried to get away by train and we had to walk. That night, before we continued on our way, we slept under the trestle of the train tracks. I remember it well because it was made of wood and it shook and trembled when the train passed over my head. I remember also because I was cold, hungry, and scared.

But being in America gave me a different fear. In Korea I knew I was going to the city of Taegu, and it felt good to be with my Korean father. But on the train I didn't know where I was going. My new daddy tried to ask me things, but I couldn't understand. I just sat there and didn't try to talk to him.

At first I couldn't tell night from day. Then we had eggs and bacon. It was good. When I was at the center for the blind in Korea, we ate meat only on special occasions, like New Year's Day. Once I remember we had beef soup. It was horrible. I gagged on a big piece of gristle and spit it out. I don't like soupy stewed meat! But the bacon on the train was different. It not only tasted good, it told me when morning came.

After a long time I heard the word "Chicago." I knew it was a famous city like New York, but I still didn't know where I was. It didn't mean a thing to me except when we got off the train. It was windy and cold—not as cold as it had been in Korea just before leaving, but windier.

After getting off the train some older people met us. I was to find out they were the Grandpa Wickes. We got into a car—my first car ride in America—and I didn't know how to tell them I get carsick! After a few minutes I threw up all over my new mother and everybody. I guess they cleaned it up because Mom held me in her arms. So I slept—sort of rested all the way from Chicago to Lafayette and Dayton.

It was a strange sleep because I had weird dreams, dreams of dogs and roasting grasshoppers, of seesaw and rice cakes and *kimchi*. Of my father, who gambled and came home drunk and argued with my mother. Of my grandmother, who made noodles and pulled my mother's hair. Of my older sister, who got mad at me for looking in the mirror and using her makeup powder. Of the sound of plopping when my younger sister fell into the river. And of living in my little house beside the rice paddies—before the war, when days were happy and I could see . . .

"Eun Jooni, stop looking into my mirror! And stop using my white powder from the flowers. I told you that you would die if you used my things!"

"No! No! No!" said three-year-old Kim defiantly to her older sister, Eun Suk. "This is Tano Festival Day. I want to wear my red dress. I want to look pretty like you. Am I not a cute little dolly? And look, today I still live. Yet yesterday you told me I would die!"

"You are spoiled and as conceited as you are stubborn," said Kim's ten-year-old sister. So saying, Eun Suk administered an awkward but firm corrective on Kim's tiny posterior. Fighting back the tears, Kim raced out of her small rice thatch house into the front street. She wanted to pout, but then she heard it—the rhythmic clicking of metal scissors opening and closing—and all hurt vanished.

"The taffy man, the taffy man!" she cried.

He was an old man and his beard was stringy white. Except for his rubber shoes, the taffy merchant looked like a sage from the Yi dynasty. His jacket was short, loose-fitting, unpressed, and buttonless. He tied it with a single bow. His baggy trousers were like his jacket— white and unpressed—and they were gathered at his ankles with red and green bands. Over all this he wore a large pocketed vest. And on top of his wrinkled brow sat a high-crowned hat made of lacquered horsehair. It didn't matter that the hat was designed to accommodate an old-fashioned topknot which he didn't have—he was Korean and his dress proved it. Besides, this was a day for all to dress in their finest. It was Tano, and along with New Year's Day and Chusok (Thanksgiving Day), Tano was the biggest holiday of the year.

Kim didn't understand the full significance of this day. She knew only that Tano was the same as her birthday, the fifth day of the fifth month. She knew also that it was a day to eat a special Korean rice bread made with dates, chestnuts, and red beans. And because this was the first day of summer and her birthday, Kim's father bought her a small piece of taffy—with a minimum of persuasion from Kim! Chewing contentedly on her taffy, Kim watched the old man push his battered cart down the dirt road to another house.

It was true—Tano was a day for merriment. The prettiest maidens of the village dressed in picturesque multicolored traditional dresses and vied for top honors in the swing contest. Thirty-foot swing standards were wrapped in Maypole fashion with colored paper, and Kim loved to watch the young girls swish high and low, then higher and higher against a clear blue sky, trying to kick a suspended bell that seemed tantalizingly near, yet too high to reach easily.

There were also wrestling matches, music plays, and dancing parades to gladden the heart of any little girl. And at night there was a feast of good things to eat. But because this was Tano, there would be a visit to the ancestor's burial ground, plus a visit to the village Buddha, where her family would offer rice cakes, vegetables, and fruit.

It was this offering of food that puzzled Kim. She couldn't understand why her parents would give good food to such an ugly statue when food was often scarce in their home. But her thoughts were interrupted when she and her family and other villagers began walking around the perimeter of a large bonfire which had been built in the square. In the shadows cast by the pale orange light, a *shaman* (fortune-teller) pounded drums and chanted scary songs. Like the giving of food to the Buddha, this ritual also puzzled Kim.

What she didn't know was that there is little uniformity of religious belief and practice in Korea. In the same family a mother might be a Buddhist and the father a follower of the Confucian ethical system. And covering all this, both family members could be involved in a variety of century-old systems of nature worship.

Kim's rural community in the province of Seoul, thirty miles south of the capital, was typical of most Korean farming communities. It was a community where village elders erected devil posts on the outskirts of the village to guard against evil spirits, a community where shamanism was an important part of the Tano festival.

On this particular day, the shaman (who is almost always a woman and frequently blind) performed her rites of exorcising evil spirits, invoking the gods for good fortune, and praying for rain and good crops. All of this was done in full view of Kim, and it frightened her.

When the shaman's performance ended, Kim's father, mother, and paternal grandmother, as well as Kim and her two sisters, returned home. Knowing that her mother's good-tasting kimchi and rice cakes would be waiting for her kept Kim awake during the long walk home. Distinctly Korean, kimchi is made by placing Chinese cabbage, radishes, red and black peppers, onions, and garlic in a crock filled with salt water and allowing the mixture to ferment several days. To this day nothing excites Kim's taste buds like a bowl of kimchi.

Perpetually inquisitive and interested in everything around her, Kim helped her mother roll out the *yo* (mattress) and *ibul* (quilted comforter) onto the hard, smooth clay floor. Wriggling like a playful puppy under the comforter, Kim tried to find the warmest spot on the floor—a position she had to fight for with the other members of the family, since they all slept on the same mattress under the same quilt.

Just as kimchi is unique to Korea, so too is the *ondol* (under-floor radiant heating system). Borrowed from the Chinese more than thirteen hundred years ago, the unusual heating system has been modified to become uniquely Korean. Hot air is conducted from the floor-level kitchen stove or fireplace through smoke flues which are imbedded in the clay or cement floor and are joined to a chimney at the opposite end of the one-story house. To ensure that no smoke escapes, several layers of newspaper and oiled Korean paper are pasted over the floor. This produces an effective heating system and an ingenious way to conserve fuel.

This principle was well-known to Kim: she knew that the floor was the place to be on chilly nights! And especially after a long festival day, the warm floor, a full tummy, and a snug *ibul* made sleep come quickly. But just as she began to doze, she heard her grandmother's voice.

"Be silent!" said her grandmother. "It is not the place of Korean wives to tell their husbands what to do. If my son wishes to go out with the village men, that is his right."

"You know we are poor only because he drinks too much," said Kim's mother, "and also because he gambles all our money on Mahjongg."

Too young to fully understand the significance of the argument, Kim drifted off into a delicious sleep to dream of pretty girls on swings. Unknowingly, it was to become a dream that lasted a lifetime. Never again would her physical eyes see the brightly colored swing standards of a Tano festival.

2. Hot Sand and Darkness

When it came, it came suddenly and with devastating force. On June 25, 1950, a Sunday morning, without warning or provocation, the North Korean Communist military forces crossed the 38th Parallel to begin the bloodiest thirty-seven months in Korean history.

Chosen by the Allied Military Command to temporarily facilitate the 1947 Japanese surrender, the 38th Parallel became, in the minds of North Korea's People's Committee, an intolerable boundary. After erecting their own iron curtain, the North Koreans accused the South Korean government of strangling the flow of consumer goods and raw materials in both directions. In an effort to "unify" the country, the North Korean government, supported by two hundred thousand smartly equipped fighting men, decided to enforce its dictatorial rule on that warm Sunday in June.

Three days later, on June 28, the Communist army rolled into Seoul on camouflaged Russian-built T-34 tanks. With amazing swiftness, the advancing army pushed the poorly equipped ROK forces back down the Korean peninsula—right past Kim's front door.

They were finally stopped near Pusan, Korea's second-largest city. Three months later, after that now-celebrated Inchon landing, United Nations troops surged northward—right past Kim's front door—to retake the capital city of Seoul.

In the meantime, Kim and her family became part of the millions of Korean civilians—men, women, and children—caught in the nightmare of a seesaw war.

Yet for Kim's mother, the war was almost an anti-climax. For years she had waged her own war against her husband's drinking and gambling. As a Korean wife she was bound by traditional ethics to be obedient, faithful, and cooperative to her husband and his parents. Under Confucianism, grandparents are the superior members of a household and must receive absolute obedience. It was to her grandmother that Kim was taught to give the first bow of the morning.

So it wasn't strange for Kim to see her grandmother reprimand her mother one day shortly after Tano by giving her hair a sharp pull. It was, however, unusual for Kim's mother to retaliate.

"You pull my hair now and tell me to not argue with my husband," she said, "but where will the winter kimchi come from?" Then with a voice full of pain and tears she cried, "Last night my husband came home full of *yak-ju*, drunk. But what is worse, he gambled all our land. We have no money and now not even land to grow vegetables and rice, and the kimchi pots are almost empty!"

With these new turn of events, Kim's mother broke with tradition. Until now she, like millions of her counterparts, relied almost completely on her husband for the economic well-being of the home. Forced by her husband's instability, Kim's mother tried to make a few *won* by selling undersized muskmelons. Her efforts were almost a total failure. And then came June 25, and nothing mattered anymore.

In a few weeks all that Kim's mother watched over would become as blasted and fragmented as the bomb-scarred cities and countryside. First it was their food. What little kimchi was left in the big clay pots stored under the eaves of their tiny two-room house was taken by the advancing North Korean soldiers.

Next, their tranquil, well-ordered community became an armed camp. After the initial push eased, soldiers in charge of ammunition supplies and communications bivouacked in the fields immediately surrounding Kim's house. Mothers in the community, who considered the Northerners uncouth and barbaric, dressed their teenage daughters as boys in an effort to keep them from being raped.

Yet all this was lost to Kim. She knew only that it wasn't as easy for her and her sisters to play with their girlfriends as it used to be. But her curiosity for the camouflaged trucks and tanks, and the flash of the high-intensity light from the bombs, more than made up for not being able to seesaw and jump rope.

"It is the responsibility of older sister to care for younger children," complained Eun Suk to her mother, "but looking after Eun Jooni is hard. Always she is stubborn. Every time airplanes fly over she runs outside to see them. She likes to see the light when a bomb explodes."

"You must make her obey," said Kim's mother. "Spank her if she won't listen. It is important to make her lie down if you are in the fields when the bombing planes come."

But Kim's curiosity was always stronger than the punishment she received. Even on the day of the air raid, Eun Suk had to drag her inside the house.

The United Nations push to drive the Communist forces off the Pusan Perimeter began on September 16. Twelve days later the North Korean army was shattered. So, too, was Kim's eyesight.

For weeks she and her family had heard the heavy drone of the famous B-29 super-fortresses plowing through the skies on their systematic missions to bomb North Korean airfields. There were no airfields in Kim's community, but there were munitions dumps, and the bombardier had his orders. He could have come from Georgia,

Wyoming, or California—from a family that espoused the all-American virtues. He could have been an Eagle Scout pledged to protect old ladies and little children. But war is hell, and he pressed the button.

"Quickly, lie down! Cover your head!" That was all the time Eun Suk had to instruct her precocious sister after dragging her inside the house. Eun Suk and her mother, father, grandmother, and youngest sister fell face down on the hard clay floor. But not Kim! She stood up and watched.

In an instant it was over. A thunderous wave of gaseous light erupted across seventy-five yards of rice fields and straight into the retina of Kim's tiny black eyes. It was as if someone had sprayed her eyes full of hot sand—as if she had been awakened in the blackness of a winter morning by a gigantic searchlight. But then, just as suddenly, all was darkness and Kim slumped to the floor. For what seemed forever, the little family lay under the dust and straw of their demolished thatch house. The bomb blast did what it was supposed to do—air pressure, sudden and terrible, blew off the roof and crumbled the mud walls of the little house.

Almost afraid to move their muscles, Kim's family slowly picked themselves off the floor. They were dazed, but miraculously no one was hurt—or so they thought.

"Eun Jooni, Eun Jooni," called her mother softly, "get up, the bomber plane is gone." There was no response. Kim lay face down, breathing but unconscious. Gently Kim's mother knelt, picked her up, held her close to her breast, and rocked her back and forth. Through her silent tears she hummed a Korean lullaby . . .

He justified his action on the basis of circumstances. After all, he reasoned, it had been three days since the air raid. The house, except for the skeleton of a wicker lattice frame, had been destroyed. There was no food. And for some unexplainable reason, his second daughter was blind. She said she could see faint light and shadow, but her family knew she was blind even though they didn't know how it happened, since no one else was hurt when the bomb exploded.

"We will have to give Eun Suk to be a house girl," said Kim's father to his wife. "I have a friend who has a friend who wants one. She will be better off. And I need the money to feed the rest of my family."

The decision by Kim's father to send his oldest daughter to work as a house girl was rooted in a long tradition of Korean history. As late as 1907 individuals could buy slaves from people who felt that the burden of normal family responsibility was too heavy. Yet to this day, Eun Suk is bitter toward her father. She has never forgiven him for separating her from Kim and the rest of her family and for sending her to the house of a complete stranger.

We all left in the back of a bumpy truck. We had nothing to take. Everything was bombed. Eun Suk was sad to say goodbye, and I cried when we left her at this strange house.

As sad as Eun Suk felt, she was, as her father had predicted, better off, for the following weeks and months became for Kim, her younger sister, mother, father, and grandmother, like the war itself—a nightmare that wouldn't go away.

After the North Korean army fell apart, the advancing United Nations forces took the northern capital of Pyongyang on October 19. Flushed with victory, the U.N. forces then pushed on to the banks of the Yalu River and the border of Communist China. Their victory, however, was short-lived. On November 24 a new war broke out. Communist China poured thirty divisions across the Yalu River. On January 4, 1951, Seoul was once again in the hands of the North

Koreans. Two months later, on March 14, the United Nations forces retook Seoul for the last time.

These war-filled months were the hardest for Kim and her family. They became part of the several million homeless refugees who wandered from community to community looking for food and shelter. Most of the communities that normally had tons of radishes and Chinese cabbages ready to be prepared as winter kimchi now had almost nothing in their markets.

After we left my sister Eun Suk, my grandmother strapped me on her back and we walked a long, long way into the mountains. After what seemed many days, we all came to live in a tiny dirt hut by a stream. There were no more bombs, so for a while I was happy just to be with my parents. Since I was now the oldest sister, I took care of my younger sister, even though my eyes were blind. I liked my little sister and we played by the water. I also helped my mother care for my grandmother, who by now had become very sick.

We didn't have much food and my mother cooked frogs to eat. Sometimes we caught crickets and grasshoppers. These we roasted on the wood fire. They were crispy and tasted good.

And then we were only four. My grandmother died and my father put her into a rice sack. Some men came and took her away. After that we left the place by the river and the tiny dirt hut and came to some towns to beg for food. I knew they were towns because the streets were narrow and crooked, and there were many, many people.

We walked and walked day after day in rain with no shoes and cold mud going up through my toes. I was cold and sad, and very hungry, and I knew my parents were worried.

Kim sensed her father's distress but didn't understand why. True, she was homeless, hungry, and often sad, yet she was still part of a family. When she slept, even on the streets, it was in her mother's arms, and however fleeting her life, she felt secure.

But her father did not. The devastation of war, severe stress, fatigue, and the exhaustion of trying to find food where there was none, panicked him. He aroused his family one morning when the moon was still shining. They had spent a fitful night trying to sleep on the cold dirt floor of an abandoned barn. Except for the inside skin of a discarded egg shell, Kim had eaten nothing for two days.

It was early when the four of us got up to begin our day of begging. In silence we walked along a narrow country road with high grass and water on one side. The moon was out, and though my eyes were blind I still saw shadows, and it made me happy to faintly see the moon's reflection on the pretty water.

The seeds may have been in his mind for longer than he wanted to admit, but he was unsure of how to do it. Or it may have been a mad impulse of the moment.

Suddenly my father stopped walking and told me to stand in the middle of the road. At first I didn't understand why. Then I heard a truck. "It is useless to go on living," said my father. "We will all stand here and let this truck run over us." I stood there and heard it coming—closer, closer. Something on the truck made a large clanging noise. I didn't know what it was. It sounded to me like a long, sharp metal bar hanging in front of the truck. I thought the wheels of the truck would miss me, but not the clanging bar. I was afraid.

Then I heard my mother scream, "No! No!" and she pulled us to the side of the road. I felt the wind of the truck on my face.

I heard the desperation as my father said, "If not the truck, then the river!" My sister's scream was followed by a heavy plunk and a splash. Before I could cry out, my father's hands gripped my legs and shoulder, and he swung me hard and let go.

3. Every Day the Same

*J*ust as Kim's relaxed resilience saved her from the full fury of the bomb's concussion, so now it saved her from the full fury of her father's explosion of stress.

I don't know why, but somehow I wasn't scared. I heard my mother scream from the bank. "No! Don't throw her, don't kill her! Get her back! Get her back!" I swallowed a lot of water, blew some bubbles, floated a bit, and hit a rock, but I wasn't scared. Then I felt the same hands that threw me into the water pick me up and carry me to the bank.

My father left me there spitting up the water I had swallowed. He went back into the water for my little sister. It was too late. She was drowned dead. And then we were three.

Because she was a Korean woman, she knew her status was lower than her husband's. And except for an occasional well-placed remark about his gambling and drunkenness, Kim's mother tried to be the right kind of wife to her husband. But whatever feelings of respect or affection she may have had for him died with her youngest daughter.

In turn, Kim's father knew that the abuse of his children would go beyond his momentarily unfocused rage. In that mad instant he lost forever not only a child, but his self-esteem and whatever prestige or social status he may have had. For as long as he lived his wife would be a living reminder of his weakness and failure to sustain Korea's most important social unit—the family. His only solution was to remove the reminder by sending her back to her parents. Overwhelmed with grief and hatred, Kim's mother left—alone.

She said she was going by herself to look for food because it was too hard to beg for three. I said goodbye and she went away. I never saw her again. And now I was alone with my father. We started to walk into town, just we two.

Before the war Korea's only urban centers were provincial capitals and county seats. Most were characterized by narrow, crooked streets, closely packed buildings, and one-story tile-roofed dwellings which were ages old and crowded with humanity.

It was here, reasoned Kim's father, that they stood a better chance to find food. And for a while they did—bits of rubbery whale meat, dried octopus, and whatever rice they could beg, find, or steal. And then the bombing started again—screaming, shattering bombs that left most northern communities in South Korea totally devastated.

This was a scary time for me. Before, when I could see, I had a house to run into. Now I had no house. When the bombs exploded there was no place to run. I held my father very tight. I liked my father, I really did.

When the bombs came, Kim and her father moved on, joined by thousands of others trying to escape the insanity of war. A great many of the refugees were farmers who plodded along as dejected and heavyhearted as the draft oxen and water buffalo they led. Others were shopkeepers and artisans who pushed two-wheeled carts loaded with the simple remnants and tools of their trade. Others were old men carrying everything they possessed on *chiges* (A-frame packboards). But most were like Kim and her father—homeless refugees who pleaded for scraps and slept where they found themselves. They became beggars, hair matted with dirt, feet blistered, owning nothing but the garments they wore—dirty, tattered, clammy with sweat.

It was impossible for Kim to tell where she and her father were going or how long they walked. Days melted into weeks and weeks into months. They begged, slept, walked; then slept, walked, begged, until Kim couldn't tell day from night and every day seemed the same. For a hundred and eighty miles they walked! Endless hours they walked over countryside so rugged that one early missionary described the country as a sea in a heavy gale.

As pointless and endless as their journey seemed to Kim, her father actually had a plan. It was rumored that the southern city of Taegu was relatively free of devastation and had a greater supply of food. But more important, he had heard about missionaries there who looked after and cared for orphans and blind children.

It was this care that occupied the mind of Kim's father almost as much as the need for nourishing food. After the superficial tissues of Kim's eyes were burned by the intense heat, a secondary infection began to set in. He and Kim didn't understand why or what was happening. Kim only knew that, when she perspired and salty sweat seeped into her eyes or when the sun shone too brightly, her eyes became infected and puffed up like eyes on a toad.

There was also the question of caste. Though Korean society has not openly practiced a caste system since the beginning of the twentieth century, Kim's father knew that a strong social pressure still placed people in rigid social molds according to occupational rank and heredity.

As a farmer, Kim's father belonged to the commoner's class.

Above him was the *Yangban* or leisure class—people of learning and high social rank. There was also a third class, below the commoners, simply called the lowly. Butchers, domestics, shamans, public entertainers, and blind people were some of those who made up this despised minority.

Traditionally, the blind in Korea were considered a disgrace to their families and were scoffed at by school authorities and rejected by family and society. Kim's father felt that when the war ended and life once again became normal, there would be no occupation open to his blind daughter except that of a fortune-teller or a night-walking street masseuse. In an effort to both relieve himself of parental responsibility and have his daughter cared for medically and physically, he led Kim to the gate of a small tile-roofed building.

When we reached Taegu my father told me he was going to leave me with people who would know how to care for me, that I would be better off than being with him. But I didn't want him to go. I had been with my father for a long time. I had no one else and I like my father. "No! No! Don't leave me!" I pleaded. "My little Eun Jooni, you will be better off here," he said as he placed two persimmons in my hands. He knew how much I loved persimmons! Then he left.

Again I begged him not to leave. This time I cried and screamed. Just as I did, loud sirens began. They came from all around me. I was frightened and confused.

Someone tried to hold me but I ran away from them. I didn't want to be left alone without my father, without any family. I ran out into the street crying for my father, but he was gone. And I was alone, completely alone.

I felt a hand on my shoulder, and someone led me into the house. I sat in a corner, a great emptiness in my stomach. I didn't know anyone; I had nothing to do; I didn't know night from day, and I cried.

The sirens Kim heard were nothing more than electrically operated timepieces. Twice each day, at twelve noon and midnight, the citizens of Taegu noted the time of day or night by this wailing signal.

As for the house where her father left her, it was a home for deaf and blind children—one of twenty-seven homes in Korea run by World Vision, and Kim was just one of more than two thousand children this mission organization was to house and care for as a result of the Korean conflict.

> Those first days in that new home were a great puzzle to me. I knew there were many other children around me, and there seemed to be only a few people to look after them. So I just sat silent in a corner and waited until I heard signs of food. Then, like everyone else, I cleared my throat. I wanted the people passing out the food to know I was there.
>
> At night I slept on the floor with other children, but it wasn't a warm *ondol* floor like I had in my little house. It was cement and very cold.
>
> Soon I had a friend, Lee Song Suk. She was six years old and just about my size. Most of the time we sat together in a corner and pinched each other. We also became competitors for food. Both of us tried to clear our throats louder than the other!

Unknown to Kim, the World Vision home for the deaf and blind was only an intermediate home. Within a few weeks after her arrival, she and four other blind children were taken to what later became the Chung Ju Home-School for Blind Children.

Aware of the special problems which blind children face in Korea, in 1952 Presbyterian missionaries Harry and Mary Hill founded a school-home solely for blind children.

> Lee Song Suk went with me and I was carried piggyback by a deaf boy to this smaller home. I enjoyed the piggyback ride. It was the first pleasurable moment I had since Tano, when I could see.

This short piggyback ride was for Kim the beginning of a whole new life of pleasurable moments. With just five children, the Hills and their staff teacher, Miss Chong Syn Yang (herself blind), had time to care for the children's individual needs. Their first and immediate need was a bath and clean clothes.

> There were four girls and one boy. His name was Moon. Miss Yang took all our clothes and we all sat under a blanket while our clothes were being washed and dried. Moon sat by me. When I heard the laundry sound it reminded me of home. For fun I had often gone to a stream with my mother, where she had washed our clothes. She put wet clothes on a flat rock, squished out the water, and pounded them with a flat stick. When all the women pounded, it made a nice sound to hear. Then the clothes were dipped again in the river, folded over, squished, and pounded some more. After pounding, my mother had hung the clothes to dry on bushes near the river. When they dried they always smelled good. And when Miss Yang brought my clean clothes back to me that first day at the home, they had a good smell, like they had been washed in the river and dried by the sun.

Just as the sounds of washing clothes triggered a pleasant memory for Kim, so did all the other sounds and smells of the well-run home. They were smells she had nearly forgotten, like pumpkin soup made from dried pumpkin slices, and homemade noodles, the kind her grandmother used to make from rice and wheat, rolling the dough out on a flat rock—flat noodles that her grandmother used to cut and hang out to dry. For the first time since her long, torturous walk to Taegu, Kim wanted to remember.

As a hungry beggar on the streets it had been too painful for Kim to remember what life had once been like. Now at long last she believed everything was going to be all right. She knew because Miss Yang's voice was soft and kind, she had eaten a large bowl of rice, and happiest of all, she went to sleep for the first time in two years on a warm *ondol* floor covered by a snug *ibul.*

Kim was almost correct in believing that everything was now going to be fine. She was right about Miss Yang—Miss Yang was kind and loved Kim immediately. Also, it didn't bother Kim one bit that she was given household responsibilities. She was, after all, five years old now, and even at an earlier age she had once been responsible for her younger sister.

Later, as others came to the school-home, they worked in teams which rotated their responsibilities weekly. Team A set the small, calf-high tables and refilled the rice bowls. After each meal, Team B swept and mopped the floor clean of fallen rice. Team C's responsibility was to sweep the long wooden porch and man the outdoor water pump. This team had the fun of pumping water through a wooden aqueduct to the cook and into pans of water for each child to wash.

Kim loved every minute of it. She enjoyed the discipline of knowing exactly what was expected of her and what her duties were, and the challenge of memorizing each routine. She was also given the responsibility of leading older children who could not memorize as quickly as she. When Kim's father placed her in the first home he had told the administrator, "Eun Joon's head is good." Within a short time Miss Yang, the Hills, and others were to understand just how good Kim's head really was.

There was, however, the immediate problem of her eyes. Along with the other children, Kim was scheduled to begin learning Braille and other subjects. But Miss Yang and others were concerned about what to do with her eyes, which kept swelling and running with matter.

One night the people in the orphanage at Taegu sat with me in a circle. They asked me if the light was on. It was just a small kerosene light which sat on top of a stand. I knew they wanted to tell how much I could see. I would like to have said I could see it, but all I could see was a faint shadow.

"Eun Jooni," said Miss Yang, "we think it will be better for you if the doctors take out your eyes." I may have started to cry because Miss Yang said she had some nice crisp pears as a treat for me. Then she said I would be prettier if the doctors took out my eyes and I would no longer have pain from the sun.

So they took me to the hospital and fed me some horrible, thin broth. Next they cut my eyelashes. I guess the doctors thought they were too long and would get in the way. One of the nice things about the hospital was the bed. This was the first time in my life that I had ever slept in a bed. I think this was one of the reasons I wasn't scared. I just kept thinking about sleeping on a bed.

It was in the morning when they took me to the operating room. They put me on a table. The head was higher than the foot and a nurse put a cup over my mouth and nose. She told me to count to ten. I always wanted to do everything right but I slowed down. As hard as I tried, I never made it to ten.

When I woke up they had it done. To my surprise, both my eyes were gone. For some reason I thought they were only going to take one, the left one that swelled the most. But they took both of them. I felt weak and threw up when the doctor came to move me.

After I returned to the center for the blind, I tried to walk from where I slept to the outhouse. I wanted to see if I could still see light. In my imagination I tried to see the stars, but people told me I couldn't see anymore. I was depressed. All of a sudden I felt like I was behind a wall. If I knocked hard enough I thought it would fall down.

It was like I had something caught in my throat, like I was hoarse. If I could cough and clear my throat, it would be all right. But I couldn't. As hard as I tried, the wall was still there. So after a while I stopped trying to knock it down. I knew there was much to do and learn and I didn't want to miss anything that was going on. Life was too exciting.

4. No Such Word as Can't

The smallest squatted on their heels as only Orientals can. Others sat cross-legged in front of still others who stood tall, straight, and smiling. It was, after all, an important milestone, and the Hills wanted their supporters to know the Chung Ju Home-School for Blind Children had progressed in four years. The year was 1956, and it was time for a "family" photo.

The caption under the photo in the bulletin read, "We're now a happy family of thirty-four and soon will be joined by twelve more in our new home." There had been previous bulletins telling of the move to a new and larger two-story facility in the city of Chung Ju, about one hundred miles northwest of Taegu. Along with the photo of staff and students, the bulletin introduced some of the students and their accomplishments.

"A few nights ago an audience of a thousand craned their necks to watch little Eun Jooni step up onto the platform with her Braille Gospel of John. As her clear, confident voice went out over the loud-speaker, the audience gave a murmur of amazed delight.

"Her reading was remarkably well-phrased and meaningful. The visiting Korean pastor stood up from his seat to watch Eun Jooni's small fingers slide without hesitation over the raised dots. This was the first time he and most of the audience had ever heard or seen a blind person read.

"As Eun Jooni read, Miss Yang and the other members of our staff thought back four years to when Eun Jooni's father first brought her to the orphanage. She was blind, motherless, and suffering greatly from malnutrition. The ravages of war had forced Eun Jooni and her father to pursue a life of begging and wandering.

"Today she is a sturdy nine-year-old, exceptionally bright, bubbling over with fun and energy. Whether it's a game of tug-of-war, jump rope, or a problem in arithmetic, she attacks them all with zest. The word *can't* is not in her vocabulary."

What the bulletin didn't explain was Kim's insatiable appetite for learning and her impatience with teachers who didn't, couldn't, or wouldn't teach her fast enough. Shortly after the operation on her eyes, Kim discovered that some of the older girls were learning to knit and she wasn't.

I was small and the teacher wouldn't teach me, so I followed Miss Yang and the cook around begging them to teach me how to knit. Finally they did! It wasn't long before I was knitting sweaters, woolen socks, hats, and gloves.

In addition to learning to knit, Kim lapped up Braille like a thirsty camel. Next she attacked and mastered the abacus with equal facility. (Korean students begin calculation with the abacus before high school to prepare for annual interschool and intercountry competition.) With the same mental dexterity she used in learning Braille, Kim quickly polished off her first- and second-grade work in short order. For her third grade, the Hills decided that Kim should be placed in a Korean elementary school.

Since most of the schools and hospitals in Korea were started and are still run by missionaries as an expression of love for Jesus Christ, the Hills considered the school an extension of their own work in the orphanage at Chung Ju. From that moment on, however, Kim's life began to read like *The Perils of Pauline*.

Returning home from school one afternoon, Kim confidently made her way along a narrow dirt road. Suddenly, from out of nowhere, she heard the blast of a horn. (Kim had not divulged the incident by the river. The Hills only knew that she was mortally afraid of moving wheels, which they assumed to be normal for a blind person.) Because cars were rare and unexpected on the road between the school and the orphanage, the horn startled her. With reflexes made of spring steel, Kim purposely ran to the left side of the road. Once before she had been startled by a car in Taegu and had jumped to the right, only to fall into a deep cement hole.

When the car horn sounded I ran fast—right into a ditch. It was an open sewer, thick like pea soup! I carried my Braille board and notes in a two-handled purse. This got full. I was icky dirty from head to toe. Miss Yang told me I needed my clothes changed more than anyone else because I was always getting dirty—getting dirty, not hurt!

This wasn't entirely true. Sometimes Kim *did* get hurt, like the time she stood singing by herself while leaning against a railing on a narrow two-tier porch.

One day I was hanging over the railing singing "What a Friend We Have in Jesus." There was another porch or landing about three feet below the porch I was on. And below that was a big drop-off of about five feet. In the middle of my song I stepped back to pull up my pants, then walked forward. But I took too many steps and somersaulted to the landing below. I landed on my head on top of a pointed rock.

I bled badly and had to have all my clothes taken off so the blood wouldn't dry on them. I went into a tiny, tiny closet and cried real loud for a long time. It must have been on a Wednesday when this happened because at night I had to go to church. The teacher put a wide band of cloth around my head to stop the bleeding. That bandage had to come all around my head like a turban. It wasn't pretty. And I still have the scar!

There is a popular belief in Korea that Korean women have an inborn talent for music. This may or may not be true. What is true, however, is that Korean women compose most of the Korean folk songs. One reason given for this curiosity is that the traditional restrictions placed on women leave few pasttimes open to them.

Whatever the reason, folk music is a deep and abiding part of Korean life and culture. Farmers sing special songs on their way to work to invoke the spirits of harvest to give good crops. Fishermen sing similar songs. Children and young girls sing with each other as they play in their courtyards and while working in the fields, and mothers sing lullabies to their babies. In all, Koreans sing more than do most Westerners and for many more reasons.

It was this cultural heritage, plus her budding talent and fondness for music, which caused Kim to accept the orphanage's nightly worship services and long Sunday and Wednesday night church services. Her interests were musical rather than spiritual, since her understanding of how to come into a living and personal relationship with Jesus Christ was confused.

We had worship services every morning and night at the home-school for the blind. I liked them because we always sang a hymn and read consecutively from the Bible. I always wanted to be a good person and one that Jesus would love. But I thought of Jesus as only a great power up above waiting to judge me for all the wrong things I did. I believed God wanted me to be obedient and do good works. Yet I knew I could not always obey even though I tried. Often I viewed myself as having to walk on a road of needles that led down to Hell and once there I would have to sit forever in fire.

I didn't understand that by faith anyone could give his heart, soul, and mind to God and become a Christian by just accepting Jesus Christ. I didn't know then how much Jesus loved me.

I liked to sing hymns but didn't like the long sermons. The young children got so sleepy they laid down on the wooden floor, fell asleep, and snored. I never did because I knew I would get into trouble, and I had trouble of another kind—I always had to go to the bathroom. Several times when I was younger I got into trouble because I couldn't hold it.

This wasn't the only trouble Kim got into at the orphanage. Like her appetite for learning, Kim had a physical appetite that wouldn't stop.

One day we all had a rare treat. We were each given a tomato to eat. When everyone finished, I went into the kitchen. Because I could get around and knew where everything was, I discovered three extra tomatoes in a big fat metal bucket. I thought it was all right, since everybody had one. But I still wanted more, so I ate one and left two.

The next day all of us (about forty) were asked to line up like we did for exercises, in lines of ten. One of the officials said, "Last night someone took a tomato from the kitchen. I want to know who did it." Well, I wasn't going to confess in front of everybody.

"All right," said the official, "all of you will be punished. You will stand in line with your arms outstretched until the guilty person confesses."

We all stood for a long time. I had big tears because my arms were so tired. But I wouldn't confess in front of people. Of course by the time evening services came I did confess—privately. I was sorry all had to be punished.

One of the more conventional forms of punishment was the writing of a theme in which one told how sorry they were for the misdeed. From Kim's point of view, this was "quite stupid." She conformed, however, preferring to save her energy to fight for what she considered a moral issue—the right of not being forced to apologize in public.

Koreans take off their shoes before they go into the house, and we had to take ours off when we went into the home for the blind. They were little rubber shoes which we placed in proper order outside the door. One day I accidently kicked someone's shoes out of order. The teacher asked me to say I was sorry. I wouldn't do it in front of the class. For punishment I was made to assume the push-up position. Others always broke down and in a few minutes said they were sorry—but not me! I was stubborn and stayed that way for an hour!

If the discipline seemed strict and militaristic, it was. The originator of the system was Mr. Shin, a former Korean army interpreter. Yet Kim, then or now, has never held bad feelings toward the orphanage.

They did it because they loved me. I never felt I wasn't loved. Even when I was once made to stand naked out in the cold, I believed they were doing what they thought was best for me. I have no bad feelings, only feelings of all the fun times I had. Not one minute was I ever bored!

I had lots of work to do, but I liked it. There was time to sing and often we sang in parts. When we didn't sing we played tag. I could tell when someone was near just by listening.

Other times I did calisthenics with the sighted kids from the elementary school, and often some there carried me piggyback.

Then there were presents from people in the United States. For my first Christmas I got a box of animal crackers. I really liked that.

Another time a package came and we all got harmonicas. These were fun to play. Once I got a soft rubber dolly with tiny little hands and feet. It was wonderful!

As for Mr. Shin, he was not all spit and polish. It was he who first recognized Kim's unusual musical gift. In the fourth grade, after all the other students had their music lessons, Mr. Shin took Kim aside to teach her additional songs and give her expanded voice lessons.

Besides giving Kim her foundation in voice, Mr. Shin instilled in her a never-to-be-forgotten self-confidence and practical working philosophy on how to live and handle herself in a world without light. He was also a wise arbitrator.

One Sunday morning I was playing with Lee Song Suk and we started to argue. I got mad at her and gave her a big push. she fell hard against the wall and hit her head. It was so loud I thought everyone on earth heard it.

"What is going on here?" It was Mr. Shin. I told him that Miss Lee was wrong. "But Eun Jooni beat me up," said Lee Song Suk. I could do that because I was stronger, quicker, and more stubborn!

Kim Wickes

"Well," said Mr. Shin, "don't you think it's wrong to fight, especially on Sunday morning?" Neither of us would admit we were wrong. It was a deadlock. "Well, then," said Mr. Shin, "let's go outside to the swing." The orphanage had built swings for us to play and have contests on, like the contests on Tano day to see who could swing the highest.

"Now," said Mr. Shin, "I want both of you to swing together." It was Mr. Shin who had taught us to do this. We would stand on the swing facing each other, with one person pumping one way and the other person pumping the other.

But now I didn't understand why he made us do this. At that moment we hated each other, and the last thing we wanted was to be nose-touching close. As soon as we started swinging I wanted to push her off. But Mr. Shin cheered us on and told us to keep pumping. Then all of a sudden both of us began laughing and the anger was gone. That was real smart of Mr. Shin!

Mr. Shin was also real smart about a lot of other things. Sometimes he would have the blind kids run relay races. We would hop on one foot or run. We even ran backward. At these times Mr. Shin seemed not to treat us like blind people. He would say, "Many people never do things because in their minds they think they can't. Remember that your mind is not handicapped."

Sometimes we would sit in a circle and Mr. Shin would say, "Now listen to this story and see if you can repeat it." Then he would describe what it was like to go to the store. "Go down the hill thirty yards. On your right side there is a ditch about ten feet long filled with mud and water. Turn left and walk twenty feet." Always he gave us great details about what we would find on these walks. I thought it was fun when we had to repeat it back to him. But I soon discovered it was more than just a game. He was teaching us how to be independent.

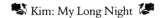
Sometimes Kim interrupted this developing autonomy as her right to outwit the teachers.

> The elementary school I went to was a good school. Many of the kids helped me during the day and came to the orphanage after school to read my assignments. Sometimes I helped them. One of these was Miss Chin, a sighted girl who liked to sit beside me. We used to cheat together. When the question was asked on a test, who did what in history, one of us would say the answer real quick to the other. If the answer was right we nudged once. If wrong, then twice.

By age nine Kim had become the orphanage's showpiece. She learned the fastest, climbed and scampered over a large nearby rock hill as if she could see, and sang like a songbird at most of the special church gatherings and evangelistic services. Because she was an inspiration for the other blind children, Mrs. Hill would have liked Kim to remain in the Chung Ju Home-School for Blind Children. But God's expanded will for Kim was soon to begin.

5. Ecstasy and Agony

Although many maps, including National Car Rental's give-away map for Indiana, don't list Dayton, it's there and has been for over a hundred years! Just five miles east of Lafayette in Tippecanoe County, Dayton, is a gentle, folksy, Norman Rockwell community of eight hundred Hoosierites.

Most lanes and back streets of Dayton are unpaved and lined with weatherworn elms, maples, and oaks. The two-story, red-brick Dayton Elementary School has a cornfield across the street from its front door. A century-old Methodist church sits at the edge of a two-block section of assorted stores and shops, the most notable ones being the white storefront post office and Robinson's Dairy Store.

During the fifties the United States reeled under McCarthyism, the flight to suburbia, and a gyrating rock and roll singer named Elvis Presley. It was a day when many back yards in America were pregnant with fallout shelters, and a beautiful fresh-faced movie star became Serene Highness Princess Grace of Monaco.

This was the beatnik age, when many West Coast young people (including some Korean veterans) became disillusioned with the old American dream of prosperity and conformity. They showed their protest by wearing khaki pants, beards, and sandals. Their Midwest and East Coast cousins were distinguished by black leather jackets, tight jeans, penny loafers, and ducktail haircuts.

But Dayton was different. The conservative retired farmers who made up most of the residents were not deeply touched by the fads of the fifties. For them, ducktails belonged on little creatures who skimmed across the south fork of the Wabash River, invaded their grainfields, and were fair game for number four buckshot.

Dayton, however, was not completely untouched by the events of the fifties. Some of its citizenry may not have understood or appreciated the subjective lyrics of a guitar-strumming folk singer in a dimly lit San Francisco coffeehouse, but Dayton's pragmatic George and Eva Wickes did understand. They may not have understood the nuances of the ballads, but they did understand the problems which some of these disillusioned veterans had created while in Korea.

During the three years of American involvement in the Korean War, hundreds of illegitimate mixed GI and Korean children were born, and by the hundreds they were discarded. Throughout many foreign subjections, the Koreans had steadfastly refused to mix their blood. The Korean mother who bore such a baby knew her child would never be accepted into Korean society.

"Isn't this terrible?"

"What's terrible?" asked George Wickes, looking up over the top of the evening newspaper.

"This article in the *Reader's Digest*," said Eva. "It says that Korean children sometimes gang up, beat, and even kill mixed-race kids."

"What's being done about it?" asked George.

"A Christian farmer in Oregon named Harry Holt heard about this in 1954 and decided to adopt eight of these unwanted orphans. When he found there were still so many more, he started his own orphanage."

"Did the Holts have children of their own?" asked George.

"Six," said Eva, then added quickly, "and we have only four! And Mrs. Holt said the Lord provided room in their hearts and home for all of them. What do you think, Honey? Isn't it kind of selfish just to raise our own four and forget about everybody else, especially when there's such need in the world?"

"Well," said George, shrugging his shoulders, "why don't you write a letter to these Holt people and ask for more information? In the meantime we'll pray and see what the Lord wants us to do."

The *Reader's Digest* article Eva Wickes read that October evening in 1956 described Harry Holt's chance viewing of a World Vision film which poignantly portrayed the tragic plight of Korean war widows and orphans.

A man of rugged appearance and action, fifty-year-old Harry Holt and his wife Bertha spent a sleepless night praying and wondering if God wanted them to do something concrete about this problem. Feeling an affirmative answer, Mr. Holt flew to Korea at his own expense and spent several weeks via Jeep and bus trekking around the countryside visiting orphanages. The following October, in 1955, after cutting miles of impossible red tape and working out the now-famous and sometimes controversial proxy adoption plan, the Holts brought twelve orphans to the United States. Four were for other families and eight were adopted as their own. From that audacious beginning, the Holt Adoption Agency over a twenty-year span has found homes for over fourteen thousand Korean orphans.

Just as the movie stirred the Holts into action, so the *Reader's Digest* article caused the Wickes to re-evaluate their priorities and ministry for Jesus Christ. It wasn't that they didn't have meaningful work to do. Eva was president of the local PTA, and both she and her husband were deeply involved in a variety of church and community projects. In addition, the door of their modest home was always open to neighbors and friends.

"Yet after reading the article," said Eva, "we wondered if God didn't have something else for us to do. I believe God gave us the gift of compassion, and we wanted to use the talents He gave us."

With a prayer that God would make His will clear to them, Eva wrote and received some preliminary information from the Holts. From the beginning, the Wickes' children, Mary Lou, Georganne, Bradley, and Brian, were included in the planning and were enthusiastic about adopting a Korean orphan. Talking to her mother one afternoon, Mary Lou injected a broader dimension into the family project. "Why not ask the Holts for a handicapped child?" she said. "Maybe even a blind child like my friend Judy."

"George, I've been thinking," said Eva one evening.

"Thinking what?" said George.

"Thinking that maybe we should ask the Holts for a handicapped child. After all, they need love too, and it must be hard to find homes for these children."

"It's okay by me, Honey," said George, matter-of-factly.

"Good," said Eva. "I'll write again to tell them we're interested in a handicapped child. We'll leave the sex and age up to the Lord."

For almost four months the Wickes waited, prayed, talked, and speculated about what it would be like to have a Korean orphan in their home. Then, when the long-looked-for letter arrived, Eva was surprised and a little frightened. It came from Creswell, Oregon, and was dated May 3, 1957:

Dear Mr. and Mrs. Wickes:

We have a little blind girl in an orphanage in Korea that we would like to place in the right home. We see from your letter of January 25 that you ask for a handicapped child and that you are leaving it in God's hands.

The letter went on to tell how Mr. and Mrs. Kinsler, missionary friends of the Hills and Holts, had heard Kim sing. Mrs. Kinsler was so impressed that she recommended that Kim, in spite of her blindness, be adopted and given an opportunity to study in the United States. The letter told of the difficult conditions which Kim had suffered before coming to the Chung Ju Home-School for Blind Children, and then it continued with this description.

Kim Eun Jeen [this was misspelled and was later to become *Jeanie*] is small for her age but will be ten years old this coming May 1957.

From the standpoint of disposition, mental ability, musical talent, poise, and balance, she is most remarkable. Her faith is utterly sincere and earnest. She is full of fun, adjusts easily to both circumstances and to cooperation with other children. Her memory is simply prodigious. She has a lovely singing voice and quick ear for music and has sung solos for large audiences, touching many hearts.

Our dream has been that she might be trained in work for the blind, as we have felt that God's hand is especially upon her for His use and glory and blessing of many.

In appearance she is attractive but could scarcely be called pretty. If she could have artificial eyeballs it would of course wonderfully improve her appearance. Her health after the first few months has been excellent.

We would ask you to pray about this. We are not asking you to give her a home. However, she is available. We feel that this is a very special little girl and pray that the Lord's will may be done.

You may write directly to Mrs. Dorothy W. Kinsler if you wish. We are enclosing her address.

Sincerely

(Signed) Harry Holt

Eva's surprise was that Kim was not part of the Holt orphanage and not of mixed American and Korean blood. Her only momentary fear was of Kim's blindness. Although the Wickes had asked for a handicapped child, they never suspected or thought that the orphanage would ask them to consider taking a blind child.

With a finger that couldn't spin the phone dial fast enough, Eva immediately called George at his work in the nearby Eli Lilly Company. "George," she said, "we got this letter—it's a girl—she's ten—very musical—but Honey . . . she's blind."

Without hesitation, George, characteristically good-natured and positive, said, "You write and tell them we'll take her. See you tonight!"

In a letter she was to write later, Eva wrote of that moment. "Since we had left the choosing of the sex and age in the Lord's hands, we did not question this. The choice was His and we were not disappointed."

There was, however, to be disappointments of a different kind. Unknown to the Holts and Mrs. Kinsler, Mrs. Hill did not share the same enthusiasm for placing Kim in a Western home. The first indication of this came in a letter from Mrs. Holt on June 19, 1957, and read in part:

We received a letter from our daughter Barbara who is in Korea telling us about a visit she had with the superintendent of the Chung Ju School-Home for the Blind. The superintendent said the Kim Eun Joon is well-cared-for where she is. That she plans for Kim to be a teacher of the blind in Korea.

The superintendent also said she wishes that if Kim goes to America it be a family that would be willing for her to come back to Korea if the Lord should lead. The superintendent is afraid that

America will spoil her with its easy life but doesn't want to ruin her chance of getting an education.

The superintendent says that Eun Joon is attending a school for sighted children and because she is so bright, was the first to attend this school. Because of her, six other blind children are also attending the school for sighted children. Because God is using her here *there is a question as to whether or not it is best to send her to the States.*

The devastating letter continued:

We see from the recommendations from your pastor, employer, and friends that you could give any child a wonderful home. However, from the above we are wondering, now that Kim Eun Joon is in school for the blind and doing so well, if it would be wise to bring her to the States.

There were additional comments about being first in line for the next handicapped child should they receive one in the next few months.

Eva and George were numb. And the second letter they received, this time from Mrs. Hill, only numbed them more. It was dated July 18, 1957.

The love in Christ which is shown in your desire to mother a blind little girl of Korea is heartwarming.

Of course you understand that Eun Joon is not a mixed-blood child, but pure Korean. In my own mind there is no question whatever that mixed-blooded children should have their chance in USA, for in most cases they are so unwanted here. I do not feel quite the same way for pure-blooded Korean children adoption.

Kim Eun Joon is happy as a lark in her present circumstances. The Christian Children's Fund will sponsor her in our Home-

School for the Blind until she passes her eighteenth birthday. She is only ten now and doesn't know a word of English.

I hesitate, not knowing what would be God's best for Kim. After forty years in Korea I am sorry to say I've seen too many Korean students lose all desire for service once they get to America. I, along with the staff, feel that many years in America would create a wall between Kim Eun Joon and her own people. . . .

The letter ended with several "what if" questions, one of which asked if the Wickes could see Kim through college should she come to the States.

Born from the same hardy, stubborn Indiana stock that first tilled the plains and protected their frontier homes from hostile Indians, this daughter of a tenant farmer did not acquiesce. In her heart of hearts she knew God had planned this unseen girl to become part of their family. Displaying her own special brand of tenacity, Eva wrote a reply to Mrs. Holt's June 19 letter.

Ever since your letter of May 3 arrived saying that Kim Eun Joon was available to us, we have considered her our own little girl. She has been the high point in our family discussions, prayers, and plans.

From the moment our other children were conceived they were dedicated to the Lord and our constant prayer has always been that they live for the glory of God. This has been uppermost in our prayers for Kim Eun Joon, too.

Eva's letter continued with several paragraphs of her willingness and desire for Kim to return to Korea should this be God's will. There was an explanation of the great sadness they all felt at the thought of not getting Kim. There was also a hint that they wished their own children would become involved in overseas Christian service. The letter then continued:

> I have always loved to teach children and I help my own with their schoolwork. I feel "Jeanie" (as we have named her) can go to public school with the help I can give her. Then, too, we have a blind lady here in Dayton who teaches music and plays the organ beautifully. She has already said that she hopes she can be of help with Jeanie's music.
>
> We feel that God led us to ask for a handicapped child. We prayed sincerely about writing you. Then, asking for one, we prayed that God would guide and direct in all that was done in finding a child for us. It is for this reason that we feel Jeanie is God's choice for us.

Because immigration quotas for 1957 were in danger of being filled by June, the Wickes requested their senator send a special bill to Congress which would allow Kim to enter the United States that year. This had been suggested by the Holts in an earlier letter and Eva was careful to point this out.

> We also received a copy of the bill our senator has introduced on behalf of Jeanie. He seems hopeful that the bill will go through. We have felt that if God wanted us to have her, He would open the way for her to come. It seems the way is being opened, but in the meantime if something happens to keep her from coming, we will believe that it is for the best. We do not know any other way but to leave it in God's hands. We feel that it has been in His hands from the very beginning.
>
> We do not want to be a hindrance to her in any way, but somehow we feel that she should have the love of a father and mother and brothers and sisters. We love her already and feel that she is ours.

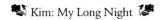

Even our little seven- and nine-year-old boys pray for "Jeanie." It would break all our hearts if we do not get to have her. However, we want what is best for the Lord's work.

We understood from your earlier letter asking us to write our senator for a special bill, that the adoption of Kim Eun Joon had already gone through. Now this most recent letter leads us to believe differently. We want her very much. We do believe all things work together for good to them that love God, to them who are called according to His purposes (Romans 8:28). We are trusting Him.

Yours in Christ,

(Signed) Mrs. George Wickes

"My little Eun Joon," said Mrs. Hill one morning in early September, "I would like to see you in my house after school this afternoon. I have some important things to tell you and I want to pray with you."

Kim had only heard rumors that she might go to America. Since they were only rumors she didn't allow herself to dream—it was too painful. After all, every child in the orphanage knew America was heaven on earth! Kim didn't really know what to expect that afternoon.

I thought I was going to Mrs. Hill's house to learn how to become a better Christian by being good, and being good included praying. After I sat down, Mrs. Hill told me about a family in America who wanted to adopt me as their own daughter. She said they had been working on the adoption since last January and now the paperwork was completed. All that remained was for me to say yes if I wanted to go.

Suddenly I had little bugs running around inside my stomach as Mrs. Hill told me this. I didn't know what to say. Then she went on.

"Eun Joon, if you go to America you will have to give up Korean citizenship and become an American citizen. This means that if ever there is a war you will have to fight on the American side. Also if you go to America, it means you will have to leave all your friends."

I was patriotic and loved Korea. All Koreans do, and I didn't like the idea of giving up my citizenship. But what I didn't like most was giving up my friends. This made me sad. We had good times together. We played hide and seek. I'd always hide in a big barrel and no one could find me. That was a good place to hide!

Mrs. Hill told me I didn't have to leave if I didn't want to. The decision was mine. "You must decide what you want to do," she said. "This is why I asked you to come. I want you to pray about what you think God wants you to do. I'll pray, too, and after we pray I want you to think about this for the next two or three days."

After Eva's June 24 letter to the Holts, and a similar letter to Mrs. Hill, the days and weeks molded into one long, suspenseful cliffhanger. The short two-block walk to the white post office became the most important and agonizing event of the day.

And then the uncertainty ended. It came on a plain half-sheet of inexpensive typing paper dated September 25, 1957.

Dear Mrs. Wickes:

After receiving the good letter from you, and then on a trip to Seoul some days later being given the Holts' letters plus the fine letters from your pastor and friends, I consulted the members of our board and teachers in the Home. The consensus of opinion was that Kim Eun Joon should come to you if this should be her desire, but that we would not send her against her will.

When we told her about the opportunity to go to America we all expected her to immediately brighten up as she had before and give a glad yes. To our amazement she said no, she could not go. But we could see that she was not happy.

I felt that the dear child did not know her own mind, that she was just naturally clinging to those she has known and loved since she first came to us. I felt she should not be hurried even though you and the Holts wanted word as soon as possible.

Sure enough, Eun Joon was not satisfied at having said no, and came to me on the eleventh of this month to say if it wasn't too late, she wanted to go to you . . .

There were further details of sending this new information to the Holts and Kinslers in Seoul to make arrangements for her flight as soon as possible. There was an apology for not having time to save Kim prior orientation into Western culture. But what the letter couldn't tell was Kim's deep agony over this most difficult of all her decisions.

6. I Will Make Darkness Light

It was almost dark when Kim and Mr. Shin arrived in Seoul. She can always tell when a day is bright, dull, or gray—she feels it. And on that cold November day in 1957, Kim felt the darkness more keenly than she had for the past five years.

The day before, a Friday, had begun like most days at the Chung Ju Home-School. Since it was November, Kim and the other students had put off using the cold wooden outside toilets until nature would no longer listen. As she pulled on her cold rubber shoes, Kim was annoyed to find little globs of frozen water that had splashed in the night before while she had washed at the outside pump.

At noon, as always, someone from the Home-School walked the half-block to the elementary school and brought Kim's lunch in a little metal box. On this day it was kimchi and rice wrapped in seaweed. Unknown to Kim, this was to be her last taste of this most delicious of all foods for many years.

After we ate, every person got a job. Some jobs the blind couldn't do, but my job was to help polish up the wooden floor. We would form a line and squat, and then with a rag we would rub candle wax on the floor until every inch was shiny. I was doing this when Mr. Shin came and said I would have to get ready immediately because I was going to go to America.

All the kids went back to their desks and the teacher of the room told them that I was going to America. Everyone applauded and told me to come back a famous person and work for Korea. I bowed to the teacher and bid them all farewell.

That afternoon I went to say goodbye to Mrs. Hill at her house at the missionary compound. She gave me a little cloth with pockets where I could put my soap, toothbrush, washcloth, and other things I would need for the trip.

Then she said, "Kim Eun Jooni, I want to give you a Scripture verse, a promise from God especially for you. It is found in Isaiah 42:16. As I read, I want you to do something. Whenever you hear the words *them* or *blind,* put in your own name. This is what the verse says:

> And I will bring the blind by a way that they knew not; I will lead them in paths that they have not known: *I will make darkness light before them,* and crooked things straight. These things will I do unto them, and not forsake them.

Contrary to what the Wickes had been led to believe, Kim did not (by her own admission) have a living, growing faith in Jesus Christ at this time. She sang gospel songs, not for the words, but for the rhythm and tune. She memorized long, complicated passages of Scripture, but it was only a game, a challenge to her quick wit—like putting together a giant jigsaw puzzle. They were words meant to be spoken with meter and rhythm. Meaning was unimportant.

Yet these words Mrs. Hill read were different. They were simple, majestic words, full of hope and meaning. They held a promise which Kim only faintly understood, but in that instant the words "I will make darkness light before *Kim"* became hers. In the loneliness and confusing moments of her life, this promise would come back to comfort and strengthen her. These were words from God, and she has never forgotten them.

That evening there was a farewell party for me at the Home-School. We had shelled peanuts and some rice cookies, but no drink. It didn't matter, it was fun. It was laughter time, not sad time. But in the morning when I had to leave and say goodbye to all my friends, that was sad, very sad.

It took almost a week for the Kinslers and Milly Holt to arrange for Kim's immunization shots and other last-minute details necessary for the November 28 (Korean time) flight. On one of the evenings, Dorothy Kinsler had Kim perform for a group of missionary ladies. But not then nor for many months to come did Kim really feel like singing.

Besides picking up a cold, Kim was almost uncontrollably home-sick for Chung Ju. Hoping to make her feel better, Mrs. Kinsler introduced Kim to a few of the eighty-six children who would be flying with her to America. Kim made friends with a deaf girl named Helen, which helped a little. Mrs. Kinsler had Kim and the other children sit in a circle to sing action choruses, but this only made Kim feel worse. It reminded her of the singing times she used to have at the Home-School, so she wept and continued to weep throughout the night.

Quiet, withdrawn, and frightened by this new experience and the many new noises and frequent sounds of cars in Seoul, Kim began to wonder if her decision to leave the orphanage had been right. On the morning she was to leave for America, Kim sat outside the Kinsler home and re-thought the events that led up to her decision.

For three days after my conversation with Mrs. Hill I didn't eat much. Usually I want more than I get, but for three days I just thought and prayed. On the last day I went to a nearby stream. The wind was gently blowing. I listened to all the sounds. I was pensive and the moment was beautiful. I love autumn—and spring too! At these times I feel close to nature.

I patted the rocks and felt how cold they were. It was early morning and the freshness of dew was all around. I threw pebbles into the stream and remembered.

A few feet from the stream was a little hill and some cement steps going up. I smiled. In wintertime I used to slide down on the side of the cement and wear a hole in my pants. Miss Yang didn't like me doing that! There was a pond nearby that froze in the winter. Miss Lee and all my friends and I would spend a long time sliding and sledding.

I loved Chung Ju and my friends, and I didn't know what to do. But the more I thought about America, the more I thought I should go. I wondered if the family in America had a pond where I could slide.

There was a last bathroom stop followed by the uncertain walk up the metal boarding stairs, and then Kim was strapped into her seat. She knew no one. Molly Holt, and her one and only link to the past and present, had tried to comfort her, but in the press of other duties she had to stay behind and was gone.

All the noise and disorder—the whir of the turboprop engines warming up, baskets of crying babies, and the sickening smell of orange juice mixed with diaper-changing odor. It was all too much. Kim again relived all the confusion, sadness, and grief of being left by her father. In Chung Ju she had become master of her environment, but now she was once again isolated, helpless, and frustrated with her blindness.

I sat by myself. When the plane took off I began to get sick. The orange juice did it. I needed to throw up but didn't know how to call anybody, so I threw up in my rubber shoe.

Later I tried to sleep, but I couldn't because babies were crying. I had to go to the bathroom but was too tired and shy to ask. Since I had left Chung Ju, I had become a different person. I was no longer happy.

In contrast to Kim's sadness, Eva and George Wickes were ecstatic. Eva recorded her feelings and the events which took place immediately before and after meeting Kim.

"As I sat with my husband aboard the plane winging westward through the winter night, I thought about another plane making its way eastward across the Northern Pacific. From almost half a world away it was bringing a new ten-year-old Korean daughter to us. The destination of both planes was Portland, Oregon.

"I wondered about what our new Jeanie would look like. There had been a delay in picture-taking, and they hadn't arrived before we left home. In a way I was glad. We felt God was giving us another child, and looks didn't matter.

"When we arrived in Portland ahead of the Northwest Orient plane from Seoul, there was a happy air of excitement among all the adoptive parents. And when the plane finally touched down, I never saw so much joy and thankfulness concentrated in one spot."

We landed in Portland and I thought, whenever I get out of the plane I will be taken immediately to my new home. I had an armband with my name and the name and address of the people who were going to adopt me. Mr. Holt came aboard the plane after we landed. He took my hand and led me out. Then he took my hand and put it into another hand. As he did he said in Korean, "Apa" (Daddy).

From this I knew I had just met my American father. And then I felt some strange wetness on my cheeks which I wiped away.

Eva Wickes continued with her journal. "When we saw Jeanie for the first time, she seemed to us like an Oriental doll with sleepy eyes. She was no bigger than a seven-year-old. I took her hand, but when I saw she didn't understand our affection or words, I prayed for God to help me ease her fear and bewilderment.

"Later, when we arrived home, her new brothers and sisters welcomed her excitedly with hugs and kisses. But, like she did to ours, she wiped them away."

When the car stopped, we all got out. I felt little pebbles under my feet. This turned out to be a driveway. We went into the basement door and up some wooden steps. This was now my home and I was there. My new family was happy. We made a circle and all prayed. Almost everyone mentioned *Jeanie,* and I heard the words *thank you, Jesus,* and *Amen.*

We had some hot tea and crackers. That tasted good! After that I sat on the couch in the left side corner in the living room. And for the next week, that was my spot.

That night Eva felt Kim would feel more secure if she slept with her, but for a long time sleep wouldn't come. Eva knew she was lonely and frightened, and as Kim sobbed Eva longed to love and comfort her, but she knew that her words, as they had been on the train, were useless. Then she remembered Kim's Korean hymn book. She couldn't pronounce the words but the tunes were familiar, and as Eva hummed one tune after another Kim finally fell asleep.

The next morning I woke up early. I heard my new dad whistle—it was cheerful, but flat! I found out later he always gets up early, whistles, and reads his Bible. When he walked I heard his hard heels click on the floor. Then I heard a squeaky tap and water.

I liked sleeping in a bed. I figured this meant rich American. It was only the third time I had ever been on a bed. Once in Taegu hospital when I had my eyeballs removed. Then once again at the Kinslers just before I left Korea.

After a little while Georganne, sister number two, came into the bedroom. (I found out later she wanted to know how I slept!) She brought in their canary. I didn't know what kind of bird it was, but I liked it. I liked it because it was a bird and because it sang. Georganne let me touch it and I liked that!

After breakfast I sat on the couch and it seemed whenever anyone passed they would hand me clothes. It was Georganne who helped most. I had a skirt, top, sweater, coat, scarf, and gloves. When I stepped outside, I thought, "Boy, they dress according to the conditions of the weather." It wasn't like this in Korea—I had only one outfit for every day, whether it was cold or not!

I didn't know where I was going, but wherever it was, it was only a short distance from the house. At first I thought I was going to school. It didn't occur to me that I would have to learn English first. I thought I would just go to school and immediately plunge right in.

The place I went turned out to be a church service with everything in English. I knew it was a church service because everyone sang. Then a preacher gave a sermon. I didn't like it. He raised his voice and I thought the sermon sounded really mean.

Kim, then and now, has little tolerance for loud-talking people. At an early age loud talking or shouting frightened her. Even now it frustrates her when people who know she is blind think they must talk loudly in order for her to hear.

Eva continued to write of her new daughter's adjustment during that first week. "Soon Jeanie was playing with balloons, dolls, and musical toys. She was very quiet but would smile at a new discovery. Occasionally I put her hand on my face and would say *Mother.* But Jeanie would not respond."

My new mother would take my hand and put it on her face and say "Mother." I knew what "Mother" meant before coming to America. I knew she wanted me to repeat it, but I wouldn't.

One day after I had been there about a week, I made up my mind I should learn English. A few days before, my father and mother gave me a new slate and stylus. They put it in front of me but I didn't know what they wanted. At first I thought they wanted me to teach them Braille. But this wasn't what they wanted me to do and their voices got louder and louder as they tried to explain. I finally got the idea that I was to write a letter to Chung Ju and I did. But that was such a scary, frustrating experience that it made me want to learn English. So I touched her and said, "Mother." I didn't like the idea of feeling or touching an older person. I had never done that before. The only people I had touching contact with were my playmates in the orphanage and my Korean father, who used to stroke my hair.

But I became happy because my mother was happy. And when all the children came home from school, my mother told them of this new event, and they were all happy.

Then all the kids began taking me around the house and letting me touch different objects. They put my hand on a table and said, "This is a table." I knew the meaning of the phrase "this is," but nobody knew this. So by repetition and rote I learned how to speak English.

Kim not only added new words to her vocabulary every day but soon became familiar with her new home and surroundings. She would open the door to the porch, find the snow, squeeze it into small chunks, and drop it down someone's back. The Wickes were delighted with her wonderful sense of humor.

"An extra one to teach, love, and care for," said Eva, "brought added responsibility for the whole family. But each child seemed willing to do his part. It seemed that Jeanie was not able to accept us all at once and would attach herself first to one member of the family, then another, until she finally included each one.

"During this time she was particularly close to her daddy. They would get up together very early in the morning, walk outside or play in the snow, then eat breakfast together. Those were precious, busy days, and our family worked together as never before."

7. New Beginnings

The first ones were made from bamboo and were designed to be used in Australia's elementary school gym classes. Then Wham-O, a California-based toy company, imported the idea and made them out of plastic, and the 1958 Hula Hoop phenomenon was born. Within six months after the Hula Hoop was introduced, thirty million American youngsters were spinning the $1.98 plastic ring around their torsos like would-be Iranian belly dancers.

Kim was one of those thirty million. At first she couldn't keep the ring spinning, but after eight solid hours of determined trying, failing, and trying again, she finally mastered the technique. For most youngsters the Hula Hoop was a once-in-a-lifetime fad that died as quickly as it blossomed. But not for Kim. Religiously concerned about her weight, Kim discovered the Hula Hoop to be an ideal exercise tool. Much to the annoyance of many of her friends, Kim today places top priority on her peppermint-striped Hula Hoop and carries it with her wherever she goes. Some people who meet Kim for the first time believe the hoop substitutes for a cane (which she almost never uses).

Hula Hooping was only one of a great number of exciting new experiences and skills which Kim mastered during her first year in America. With unusual patience and love, Eva Wickes spent hour after hour teaching her new daughter to read and speak English in preparation for the September 1958 school year. Always rising to the highest intellectual bait, Kim quickly devoured the first-, second-, and third-grade readers before school began.

There was, however, one experience that Kim then or now has never fully understood or appreciated. It's called spanking. Her most serious encounter came just after her first Christmas.

I knew Americans had Christmas, and when the tree came it smelled good. I got a doll I called Nancy, a small stuffed doggie, and some other gifts. But none of them impressed me as much as a jack-in-the-box music box which had a dog that popped up and played Brahms' Lullaby.

By now I was sleeping in my own youth bed next to my parent's bed in their room. I liked to sleep with this dog music box, and sometimes when I couldn't sleep after getting up in the early morning to go to the bathroom, I would play it.

One time Mom got really angry because I woke them up. By this time she had begun spanking me for doing naughty things, and I didn't like this. On this morning she made me turn on my stomach to be whacked on my bottom. I thought when she did this she didn't love me anymore and I wanted to go back to Korea. Besides, I wanted to play that dog!

At the home for the blind in Korea, we sometimes got hit across the legs for bad things. But we were always told how many hits we were to get and what it was for. And if we said we were sorry first, we would not be punished. Once one of my friends was put in a closet all day, but she could have come out if she had said she was sorry. People in America say this is a cruel way to punish. Yet to me the American philosophy of spanking without explaining is cruel.

While Kim was learning new things about America and herself, her parents, grandparents, brothers, and sisters, as well as the people of

Dayton, were learning new things about themselves and about so-called handicapped persons. Nearby neighbors who before Kim's arrival had wondered if the Wickes truly knew what they were getting into, ended up adopting their own Korean orphan. Another woman in the community donated money for Kim to buy a Braille Bible—all eighteen volumes!

Mr. Wickes, Sr., became so fascinated with Kim and her dexterity in handling Braille that he learned to read and write the pimple-like dots in order to communicate with his new granddaughter. It was this trombone-playing grandfather who first implanted in Kim the notion of working hard to become a famous artist. This notion, however, never sat well with Eva. Later that year, when Kim's music teacher echoed Mr. Wickes, Sr., Eva's reply was, "We do not want her to be famous, only as it will help in the Lord's work. We pray she will want to help her own people."

> I liked Grandpa. He understood how much I liked music. But Grandma was different. Whenever I would go downstairs she would say, "Don't fall, don't fall!" This would bug me.

After reading a special booklet from the Indianapolis School for the Blind, George and Eva learned how best to handle and live with Kim's blindness. Some of the rules were: "If there is a blind person in the room alone, tell him when you come in, especially if you are wearing sneakers. Same thing when you leave. Important: blind is not deaf. Don't shout. Also, blind is not dumb. If you have a question for the blind, i.e., about what he would like to eat, ask him, not his companion. Remember, blind persons are full and complete human beings; do not separate them from society. It is always appropriate to *offer* your help, but don't be surprised if he'd rather do it by himself. And when he does, it isn't necessary to applaud."

At first the Wickes children found it difficult to overcome wanting to help Kim do things. However, in a few months she was being spanked and treated like any other member of the household. She had to fight for her place in the bathroom and took part in vigorous debates as to whose turn it was to dry dishes.

While Kim rapidly learned to speak English, there were a number of words which confused her long after she was able to communicate.

> When Daddy came home from work he would always say, "Hi, Sweetie!" I misunderstood him and thought he was saying "Speedy" and I didn't know what it meant. I knew it was a good word because he always said it smiling.
>
> I was also confused about the word "dog." When my dad took me on walks to the post office, there were always dogs that came around us. Dad would always tell them to go away. Sometimes they licked my face. I didn't like that. I thought that was so dirty. Dog's just had to be dirty.
>
> At first I didn't know what dogs were. Whenever I heard the word "doggie," I thought they were saying *tokee,* which is Korean for rabbit. Then I thought rabbits in America sounded like dogs, and that seemed funny to me.

Kim had further trouble understanding the word "water," which often came out "wader." She had no trouble, however, learning to swim.

> They took me to the park to swim. It was the first time I had been in so much water since my Korean father threw me in the river. But I did not think about that. I was just scared I would sink when Dad said, "Relax and lie down." It wasn't until a few weeks later, when I had a life belt around me, that I leaned over and thought, "Ah! So this is floating!"

Once after just learning to swim I got out too far into the deep section and couldn't touch the floor. I kept trying to reach a shallower place but I didn't know which direction I should go. It seemed like an eternity I was out there. Finally somebody came and pinched me. I thought it was my brother Brian coming to wrestle me, so I pinched back and began to wrestle him. But it turned out to be a girl lifesaver. She got hold of me around the back and dragged me in. That scared me for a while, but not much.

Besides learning to swim, Kim learned to play chess, tiddlywinks, and checkers, and of course she excelled in blind man's bluff! She was also not above playing pranks on her siblings and (when no one was around) on her pet cat, Butterball.

I would lock the cat in my bedroom and rapidly turn the light switch on and off. This would drive the cat crazy! Sometimes I tried to leave the cat in the room and close the door. Then all of a sudden the cat would scratch me and dart out of the room. Several times I had cat marks all over my arms, but I was just playing.

While Kim enjoyed games and the outdoors, these were limited moments of diversion. It wasn't long before time became heavy on her hands and "What can I do?" became an often-repeated phrase. Then one day in early March all this changed.

To give Kim a new experience, Mary Lou took Kim to her afternoon typing class. For some unexplained reason, the teacher dismissed the class five minutes before the dismissal bell. These were to become some of the most significant minutes of Kim's life.

Mary Lou knew I had learned the American alphabet before coming to America and thought it would be fun for me to learn how to type.

It was! She was a good teacher and taught me the right fingering. We did it letter by letter through the alphabet. In those few minutes I learned the whole keyboard.

Kim's remarkable mental agility and physical dexterity both amazes and bewilders her friends and family. Her good friend and manager, Jim Barnes, said, "When I phone to ask Kim about her schedule, without a moment's hesitation she's able to give me five or six different phone numbers, dates, places, and plane schedules of her upcoming itinerary. She has also memorized at least a thousand phone numbers of friends all over the world and knows when most were married and born!"

Said Eva, "When Jeanie first came I never dreamed she could learn so fast or do so many things. I was told she knew how to knit but didn't know how well until I saw her doing it. She picks up stitches without any problem and knits better than most sighted people. I soon learned that if Jeanie made up her mind to do something, she could do it. As time went on we all marveled, and marveled, and marveled! We also got to the place where we realized this was just the way Jeanie was and sometimes took her for granted."

With extra money earned from tasseling corn, George and Eva bought Kim a sturdy Olympia Upright typewriter and encouraged her to practice.

When I had time to myself, which was a lot, I pecked at the typewriter to amuse myself. Mom was glad I was typing and it was fun. It was something new, like a game, and I like new games!

By March 26, Kim had progressed well enough in English and this new "game" to type her first letter to Mrs. Hill.

Dear Grandmother Hill,

We have a new typewriter. I like to type. When Daddy brought it home I jumped up and down. That was a happy day.

Spring is here and the tulips are coming up through the ground. Almost every day I go outside and see how much they have grown. I like to climb the cherry tree. I will be happy when there are cherries on the tree. I am learning to walk around the house by myself.

Yesterday Mother and I went to Lafayette, and I took my music lesson. My teacher's name is Mrs. Overton. She is very nice. She has a Seeing Eye dog. Her name is Wendy. She gave me a Braille hymn book with fifty hymns in it. I have two music books now.

While we were in town I got new Spring slippers. A neighbor lady has made me a new blue dress. Her name is Mrs. Jenkins. One day I stayed with her while Mother went to town.

One day Mother and I took a walk in the woods. We walked to the river. The river made a big noise. I threw many rocks into the water. We heard many birds. I did not want to go back home. We walked about two miles.

How is Kim Eun Yong? Is he bigger than he was when I was there? How is Grandfather Hill? I hope you are all well. I have not been sick at all.

This Friday evening we are going to Grandma and Grandpa Wickes at Indianapolis. We will stay until Sunday evening. I like to go there, but do not like to ride in the car. I still get carsick.

Mary Lou and I are going to make a cake when she gets home from school. I like Mary Lou best of all.

Love,

Jeanie

Georganne also helped Kim learn her "letters" by forming them out of play dough. And from a child's jigsaw puzzle she learned the shape, relative size, and location of all forty-eight states, though at times getting Colorado and Wyoming mixed. From another such puzzle Kim learned the Great Lakes, all the main American rivers and wilderness roads, plus the thirteen original colonies. In addition she learned to count and handle money.

Pennies don't have scalloped edges. Nickels are thicker than pennies, and dimes and quarters have rough dotted edges.

Folding money, of course, gives her trouble. She has overcome this minor problem with a secret way of folding each denomination—a secret which she does not divulge! In recent years Kim has written her congressman to ask that a special bill be passed to help the blind. she feels the problem could be solved by embossed numbers on all paper money.

By September 1958 Kim was ready and eager for elementary school. In the eyes of her observers, Kim seemed to have Americanized overnight. But it had not happened without struggle. After some minor problems in finding the right teachers, Kim was taking piano and organ lessons and even acculturating to the point where for a time she upheld the all-American tradition of resisting piano practice!

She was also taking voice lessons and had melted the hearts of her audience with the sweetness of her clear voice. But when Kim first arrived, she told her parents she couldn't sing because God was taking away her voice.

I had always sung at the Home-School for the Blind in Korea without any trouble. But when I tried to sing in English, my voice sounded different. It was hard for me to sing and I would perspire. In Korea, Mr. Shin told me if I sang easily it would be right and I would not perspire. Therefore I thought I was doing something wrong. That scared me and I said I would not sing.

With encouragement from her family, friends, and teachers, Kim overcame her hesitancy and joined the junior choir sponsored by the Wickes' Methodist church. By the end of February she made her debut by singing "Saviour Like a Shepherd Lead Us." This was just the beginning of a long line of debuts. Yet even after demonstrating to herself that God had not taken away her voice, Kim was still hesitant to sing in English. At the end of October she wrote the Hills to bring them up-to-date on her progress.

> Dear Grandfather and Grandmother,
>
> I am getting along fine in school. I started in the fourth grade but it was too easy for me. Mother talked to some of the teachers and they worked it out so I could take geography and history with the fifth grade, and arithmetic and English with the sixth grade. I still take reading, health, and history with the fourth but have finished my fourth-grade reader which I have in Braille from the state blind school.
>
> I do not have any other books in Braille, but Mother and Daddy help me write out my lessons every night. I do them with the typewriter. We have found a place in Chicago where they will transcribe all my books into Braille for next year. I have three wonderful teachers, and I like my school real well. I will be in the seventh grade next year.

One of Kim's first-year teachers was Mrs. Light, a delightful woman who is everybody's idea of what a Midwestern schoolteacher should be. Her stock in trade was an old tennis shoe, which she used liberally on the Huck Finnesque offenders in her schoolroom and on the playing field!

Said Mrs. Light of that first year: "When Jeanie first came to school she didn't have any eyeballs and we almost drew back, though only for a moment because almost instantly we fell in love with her. The other children felt the same way, too. Some almost argued over who was going to take her to lunch and the rest room!

"I loved teaching Jeanie. She grasped concepts easily and anxiously wanted to know all about everything. And when she handed in a lesson, it was typed! At night she wouldn't go to sleep until she was certain she had her assignments letter-perfect. Her great desire to learn sometimes made her impatient to move ahead. One day she said she didn't understand why all the other children were so stupid and didn't know their multiplication tables. But the other children didn't have a chance against Jeanie. She worked her abacus so fast that when I gave a problem, Jeanie had it before the other children had any idea what the answer was.

"The same was true of spelling and most of her other subjects. Not once did she feel sorry for herself. Her independence and ability to learn and excel (she went through the fourth to sixth grades in one year and played the piano better than any child I had ever heard) taught us all great lessons in how to be more understanding and sensitive to people with handicaps."

In that same October letter to the Hills, Kim explained how she walked to school with her sisters and brothers and of having a new Korean brother named Timmy.

Have you heard that we have a new little boy? He came to Portland October 9 and Daddy met the plane (just like he did for me). He is five years old and is half American. He had polio and is crippled in his left leg. The doctor thinks he can be helped with operations. He and I have lots of fun talking in Korean. I think he is smart. He knows a lot of songs. He likes our food and eats a lot like I do. Mother and Daddy didn't plan on getting him until sometime next year, but we are all glad he is here.

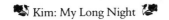

I am learning to play the Moonlight Sonata now. I played the piano a long time today (eight hours). I sing a lot more now than I did at first. I don't think my voice is as pretty as it was there. I am sending an article that was in the paper about me. You can see by the picture that my hair is curled now. May God bless you always.

Love,

Jeanie

By the end of the first school year in June 1959, Kim's adjustment to America was almost complete. At home, hamburgers and potato chips replaced her longing for kimchi. She didn't like milk or puddings but loved popcorn and pizza. The result was a gain of twenty pounds and the exasperation of her mother, who didn't know how to curb Kim's voracious appetite.

Socially she had a passel of new friends who were excited over her imported seesaw game. And because she was learning and experiencing a whole new kind of life, Eva found it increasingly difficult to persuade Kim to continue her correspondence with the Hills.

On June 9, 1959, Eva did succeed in getting Kim to write a letter that may or may not have pleased the Hills. The first part of the letter explained the differences in American schools and what she remembered of school life in Korea. Kim also highlighted special days they celebrated in school.

Difference in holiday is we have Halloween at October 31. Little children dress in funny clothes and go out at night and let the neighbors guess who they are. Then they give the children some cookies and candies. Another day is Valentine's Day. On this day people give each other a Valentine card. On it is mostly about the loving, but it is playing.

There was then a full account of the subjects and grades she had taken for that year. All were A's except for two B's—one in health and the other in science. Near the end of the letter Kim listed her new friends and told about some of the things they did.

> We had a wiener roast and hayride. We had lots of fun. When we have a hayride we put hay in the bottom of the wagon and every-body sits on the hay. The wagon is pulled by a tractor and we take a long ride singing and shouting as we go. My teacher said I made the most noise. Last night I climbed up the cherry tree and picked some (I used a ladder). In America we have swimming pools and get to have a swimsuit and go swimming.
>
> I have been to Bible school for the last two weeks. We splatter paint and some days we take a walk in the woods and play games. We are studying the Psalms.
>
> I am taking foods in Four-H Club this year and have baked three kinds of cookies, and three kinds of drinks, and three kinds of desserts and sandwiches. I help serve three family meals. I am having a slumber party this coming Friday, which is June 12. Six of my friends are staying all night!

At the end of the letter Kim confessed that she still didn't like to sleep by herself but didn't complain as much anymore. This and her fear of "come-back dead people" was the least-talked-about and most difficult adjustment for Kim and her family.

Kim had not yet told her parents about her Korean father throw-ing her into the river. Nor had she explained why she was afraid of graveyards, dying, being left alone, and of dead people returning to life. Part of this fear came from the universal childhood practice of telling ghost stories.

> In Korea when I couldn't sleep I would be scared of the wrong things

I had done during the day. Some of the girls would say that because I had misbehaved, the ghost of a person who had died would come back and haunt me. Then all of a sudden I would hear creaking and crackling noises, and in my imagination I would see the form of a person walking with only white socks. Then this form would hang on the ceiling and I would be very frightened.

Many nights after I came to America, I would think about that scary story of ghosts coming to haunt me for the bad things I had done. At first I knew my American mother and family didn't understand why I cried when I had to sleep alone. And at first I didn't understand myself. Then I also remembered that the schoolmaster in Korea would tell us the *kwisheen* (ghosts) would get us when we misbehaved.

It was true that Eva didn't fully understand Kim's fear, yet she was sensitive to it. In a letter to the Hills shortly after Kim arrived she wrote: "One thing that puzzles me a little is that Jeanie seems to be afraid of death. I talk to her about heaven and how nice it will be there, but she says, 'No. Good people go there. Jeanie bad.' I told her Jesus was the Good Shepherd and how she was one of His lambs, and she said, 'Jeanie a little lamb broke on the floor.' I don't know what goes through her little mind. We have a view of the Dayton cemetery from our kitchen window, but I haven't dared to tell this to Jeanie. She has a deep fear that dead people will come back for her."

To comfort Kim, Eva read her familiar Bible stories. Yet while Kim had memorized long passages of Scripture, she had not personally annexed the strong words of Scripture to herself. Because she had not then been made perfect in Christ's love, she could not understand the promise that perfect love casts out fear. That would take a walk down a sawdust trail and a personal interview with a piercing blue-eyed evangelist named Billy Graham.

8. The Wallflower Buds

*I*n 1945 he was cited by American Airlines as their top civilian passenger of the year. In the seventies he led the vote as the "most admired man" in the Christian world. In October 1959, Kim thought he was just an angry preacher. Yet when Billy Graham began a crusade in Indianapolis, she wanted to attend.

Perpetually curious and anxious for new adventure, Kim didn't even object to the long sixty-mile drive from Dayton to Indianapolis. She knew that Billy Graham was famous, but her real interest in going to the crusade was George Beverly Shea.

"We are all looking forward to the big Billy Graham Crusade next week," wrote Eva in a letter to the Hills. "Jeanie has great affection for George Beverly Shea. She plays his records over and over until they are almost worn out and has even copied out the words of his songs in Braille."

Kim's appreciation for Beverly Shea didn't diminish during that Indianapolis crusade, but her devotion to him was replaced.

That first night when I heard Billy Graham and he said, "You give your life to the Lord," I thought that meant only for adults. I had the impression my opinions and children were not important. In Korea it was always adults who made decisions, never children. But when Mr. Graham said, "Now *you* come, and *you* come, and make it sure with the Lord," it was like he was talking just to me.

On the way home that night I told my dad I felt like I wanted to go down to the front when Mr. Graham asked people to go forward. He said, "Jeanie, I would like nothing better than for you to go forward." This really surprised me because I thought he didn't think I was important.

The next night it was raining and the coliseum was about two-thirds full. As he was speaking, Billy Graham said, "If Jesus Christ comes back in the next thunder, would you be ready to meet Him?" That scared me, and with Bradley holding my hand, I went forward, and Jesus became my personal friend.

That simple, decisive moment was more than just an emotionally charged experience. Deliberately, and with a conscious act of her will, Kim related herself to God's purpose and will through faith in His Son, Jesus Christ. One of the first requests of her new Friend was for Him to take away her old fears.

The first winter when I found out about the graveyard so close to the house, that was all I needed! I would get terribly scared and have visions of dead people peeking through the bedroom and bathroom windows. I told Mom and Dad about this but all they said was, "People don't come back from the dead."

But I had heard all those ghost stories when I was in Korea, and now here was a graveyard so close. What else could I believe? For a while I had visions of my Korean father coming back from the dead. I thought he must be dead.

After I asked Jesus Christ to come into my life, I was still afraid. Mom told me it was a sin to be afraid, so I prayed for Jesus to help me get over being afraid—and in a short while He did!

Kim not only met the Greatest of all friends that rainy October night, but she also established an enduring friendship with the Graham team. Billy Graham first met Kim backstage one evening after the crusade to explain how she could have the assurance of her salvation.

The morning after I had gone forward, I woke up expecting to be a totally different person, but I wasn't. I began to think maybe I didn't do it right. I told my Mom and Grandma Wickes that I didn't feel different inside. When I told my dad, he thought it was important enough to take me backstage and talk with Billy Graham and some of the other team members.

Billy Graham repeated John 1:12, "But as many as received him, to them gave he power to become the sons of God, even to them that believe on his name," and he told me the change in my life would not be as pronounced as for someone who had lived in deep sin. He told me I was saved by faith in Jesus Christ and on the authority of Scripture, not how I felt inside.

In those few minutes Kim understood that within the space of two short years she had been adopted twice, once by the Wickes and now, because of her faith in Jesus Christ, into the family of God.

Cliff Barrows of the Billy Graham team would have liked to adopt her for a third time. Because Kim liked the sound of his voice (she thought it was radiant), she asked to meet him. Eva made an appointment and took Kim to meet Cliff several days later.

"I met Kim for the first time one afternoon when Ted Smith, Bev Shea, and I were practicing by ourselves in the coliseum," said Cliff. "I noticed her mother leading her by the arm. It was evident she was blind. After Mrs. Wickes introduced themselves, she told me Jeanie could sing. 'Great,' I said. 'Ted can play for her.' But Kim said, 'Oh, I can play for myself.' As she sat down I thought, 'What a wonderful smile,' and when this twelve-year-old began to sing *The Love of God,* it was too much! The power, range of her voice, and radiance of her face brought tears to us all."

In that instant Cliff Barrows became for Kim a life-long correspondent and confidant. And for Cliff and his family, Kim became a source of blessing, inspiration, and sometimes concern. Cliff still marvels at Kim's ability to maneuver through his house and "see" through her sense of touch and hearing.

"The first time Kim came into our home," recalls Cliff, "she said, 'I want to *see* your house.' She passed her fingers over the furniture and memorized almost instantly where everything was placed. Next she felt the texture of the drapes, walls, and brickwork on the fireplace. Then she touched the flowers to *see* if they were wet or dry and fingered the leaves to *see* their shape. In those few minutes I understood that what Kim feels, she does indeed see. By feel and touch she got to know our house better than our closest friends, perhaps even better than our own family!"

In 1960, September came to Dayton as it always has, with cool nights and bright orange pumpkins waiting for the inevitable frost. For most of the junior high students in Dayton, that September was a mixture of nostalgia and excitement—sadness because summer camps, swimming holes, vacations, and summer romances were ended; and excitement because a new school year meant football, basketball, and sock hops. But Kim shared little of her friends' nostalgia and excitement as she began the eighth grade.

Just as the passage of time had changed the corn shoots in the fields around the school from tender green to crusty brown, so life for Kim had changed. She was still much loved by her family and teachers, yet it was different. She was no longer a novelty.

At first her quick mental perception fascinated her sisters. Then it became, "Why do you always have to be right?" Or, "Brains won't get you everything." Kim admitted she sometimes found it strange

to always win the spelling bees or math quizzes, but added, "Most of the time I don't even try to win. It's not that I'm smarter. It just that most of the kids are lazy and don't want to work."

It also bothered Kim that most of her girl friends were more interested in spending long interludes in front of mirrors combing their hair than in paying attention to schoolwork. In Korea, attending school was considered a privilege, for only in recent years had schools been opened to girls. Because learning and school is held in high esteem in Korea, a teacher's word is to be obeyed instantly. For a long time it confused Kim when discipline was informal or when a student seemed to be disrespectful to a teacher. In Korea it was a disgrace to talk or fidget while a teacher lectured.

Her social life was also changing. Early in her school career Kim developed a fascination for basketball (later she would add wrestling), and she became an avid fan and supporter of the Dayton team. It was her voice that always came through loud and clear over the others in the cheering section. But at halftime she sat alone. It was the same during lunch hour and special social activities.

We would play records and people would dance. Those who didn't know how sat around the wall. I began to learn a new word—wallflower. I thought, "That's me" because I never got asked. I really didn't mind because I thought the pop songs were stupid. Who could care about "Oh Ma, He's Making Eyes at Me" or "Venus, Goddess of Love That You Are"!

During lunch hours at school everyone would go outside except me and a girl named Sharon who had muscular dystrophy. But I guess it was okay because then she had someone to talk to.

Social isolation was only one of the several frustrations Kim faced that September. The demands of a growing family, plus extra attention for Timmy, diverted much of the time Eva had previously spent with Kim reading school assignments. And being unprepared for a lesson was for Kim, then and now, almost immoral.

In addition to the problem of finding time to read assignments was the increased difficulty of finding people to Braille her texts. With frustration piling on top of frustration, Kim asked her parents for the change they were all beginning to realize must come—the Indiana State School for the Blind.

> After being in the eighth grade at Dayton School for a week I went to the School for the Blind. For the first time since leaving Korea I was back in a dormitory. But it was different than what I had known in Korea. Here everything was done by the ringing of the bell.
>
> There were rigid rules. I guess it was necessary. Many of the kids came from welfare homes and some were bitter about being blind. For the first time I heard bad stories—like one girl who told me she had been molested by her brother when she was five. There was another girl who always smelled bad and burped like a pig. I began to realize there was going to be more to America than just a place where there was lots of food and everyone had a house to live in.

For the first year, George and Eva drove the sixty-five miles each Friday to pick Kim up at school and bring her home for the weekend. But by the second and third years, Kim spent fewer and fewer weekends at home in Dayton. And the weekends she did come home were spent counting the hours until she could return to school. It wasn't that she didn't get homesick. She did, especially during the first few weeks. To get over this she took part in an almost abnormal amount of extracurricular activity.

Besides carrying a full academic load, Kim took piano, organ, flute, and voice lessons. Each required at least an hour's daily practice, making her day begin an hour or more earlier than that of her contemporaries. As if this weren't enough to keep her busy, Kim became secretary of her class in the eighth grade, and student council president and secretary of the Press Club in her high school freshman year. In her sophomore year Kim became editor of the school paper, president of the Latin Club, student council secretary, and captain of the cheerleading team.

She was also one of the few totally blind persons assigned to lead visitors on a sightseeing tour of the facilities. Few, however, knew that Kim was totally blind, for by now she had artificial eyes. She came away from her first fitting with one blue and one brown eye—the only ones available at the time in her size!

The other reasons for her interest in school were Bobby and Terry.

When I first went to the blind school, the woman in charge told me there was a cute boy named Bobby I should get to know. Well, I did. He just came up and asked me to go with him and be his girl. I thought this was strange, but I guess that's the way blind people had to do it.

He walked to classes with me, carried my books, and took me to the school dances and other special occasions. It was fun, but our romance didn't last too long. After a while I just had too many things to do.

Then Terry came along. He was different. He was a Christian and had a brilliant mind. I liked him. Then we broke up, too. I had heard about boys breaking their girl's heart, and when Terry stopped going with me it broke my heart. I cried all night long. It was hard to be fourteen, blind, and away from home at a time like that.

It was also hard for Kim to maintain her Christian witness, or so her parents thought.

When I first started the school for the blind, Mom told me to try and start a Bible study. I tried for a while, but there were so many regulations, activities, and regimented rules about when you could do things, it was impossible to find time. It was the same with reading my Bible. I knew it was important but I couldn't always fit it in. My folks thought I was not growing in my Christian faith. But I don't think that was so. In my heart I knew I wanted to be like Jesus and used to tell my friends about Him.

In fact, I told several people how they could come to Jesus. Beverly was one. I told her all about coming to know Jesus as her personal Friend and Saviour. We prayed together, I sang "Just As I Am," and she asked Jesus to come into her heart. We still write each other.

Then there was Eric. He was twenty, sort of funny, not always straight in the head. One night in the study room he came in and told me he was depressed because his girl had broken up with him. I told him Jesus could take care of his depression if he would ask Him. I prayed with him and he said he felt happier because his burden was lifted.

While Kim frequently affirmed her friends, there were always others who supported her during hours of confusion or decision. One of these "special" friends to come into Kim's early life in America was Dr. Al Stewart. When Kim first met him, shortly after her arrival in Dayton, Dr. Stewart was director of musical organizations at Purdue University, a position he held for forty-one years.

"After meeting Jeanie, I was immediately impressed with her as a person," said Al. "I followed her progress through the years, and when she began singing, I had her sing with the Glee Club when she could. The fellows loved her and treated her just like their little sister.

"There was never a moment when Jeanie didn't know what was

going on. One day she came into the studio and said, 'You've been eating peanuts.' I laughed and told her the last one I had was two hours ago!

"Musically she was spectacular. She sang and played the piano and organ, and each ability excelled the other. But it wasn't just technique. I've heard many great voices that left me cold, mostly because there was no personality behind the voice. This was never true of Jeanie. When she sang, the depth of her personality and character came through in her voice."

These were no idle philosophical words from a kindly gentleman. Dr. Stewart knew long before most people that Kim's combination of deep character and God-given talent would be a powerful communication vehicle, and one night he let all of Tippecanoe County in on his secret.

Following that evening, the local newspaper confirmed his feelings. Under the heading "Few Eyes Dry at Sing Finale," the article read, "The Purdue University Varsity Glee Club pulled open all the stops on its vocal keyboard in its end-of-the-year concert Saturday night. . . . About midway in the program came one of those events which strike deep at human emotions. Dr. Stewart called Jean Kim Wickes, a fourteen-year-old Korean girl blinded in the war who now resides in Dayton, to the stage to sing 'The Lord's Prayer.' In a beautiful sweet soprano voice and with the Glee Club giving background support, she sang this beautiful number with an emotional touch and musical sweetness that left few dry eyes in the audience."

As Kim moved deeper into adolescence—a process which is seldom smooth or automatic—her urge to know everything from Socrates to sex sometimes clashed with her parents' conservative views. Later there were clashes over the length of her skirts, her feeling that not all boys with long hair were rebellious, and the kind of music she often wanted to sing at church or in concert. Once some

Dayton church members considered an aria from Handel's *Messiah* too long-haired and suggested that perhaps next time she sing a more familiar church hymn.

Sometime's Kim's ideological collisions were not with her parents but with herself. As a preteen Kim depended on her acute and highly developed deductive and systematic thinking to solve problems. But now her body, moving into womanhood, pulsated with new feelings and emotions beyond the reach of logic.

There were no models with which to compare her new world of reality. Kim's Korean ancestry had given her a cultural heritage which was part of her personality. This was mingled with a Midwestern Christian ethic and subculture. In addition, she was uncertain as to how she should handle her developing talents. When Kim did decide to be a concert soloist, it was not a popular subject around the Wickes' large dinner table. George and Eva didn't want to encourage her in something they felt was a physical impossibility.

At fifteen, the only part of America Kim knew anything about was Dayton and the cloistered rooms of the state blind school. And in Dayton, her girl friends were learning to cook and sew and talked about marriage, which for many occurred shortly after high school. In a burst of abandoned tears, this mixture of anxiety, frustration, and bewilderment exploded one night after everyone retired.

I finally woke Mom up. I was in tears and told her I didn't feel normal like other kids. I told her some of the kids mocked me, made squeaky voices, and tried to imitate me when I practiced voice. I told her I wanted to be like other kids, but I didn't feel normal because when I tried to talk about intellectual things, the kids laughed at me. They said I couldn't be normal if I wanted to practice music instead of going outside to play ball or play records and talk with them.

Mom was patient and told me people truly loved me and

admired me because I was different. That didn't satisfy me, but I felt good because I had told someone, and I went back to bed contented.

By the end of her third year at the Indiana State School for the Blind in 1963, Kim's intellectual ability far outdistanced that of her peers. Her social development had also grown from what it had been in Dayton. Yet her father noticed she had a growing uneasiness around sighted people.

"I knew in order for her to be prepared for college," said George, "Jeanie needed to get out into the hard world and learn what life was really like." Wisely, he suggested a change.

9. The Pumpkin Hour

Historians could easily have elected 1963 as one of America's grimmest years. It began with the coldest winter since 1899, then the sixth-coldest on record. After a cool spring and summer, two-thirds of the nation began October with its land blistered and cracked with drought. Hurricane Flora, which careened across the Caribbean leaving six thousand people dead in Cuba and Haiti, missed the East Coast but became a prelude for the tragedy of November 22.

While the assassination of President Kennedy and other events of 1963 caused Kim as much grief and wonder as it did most Americans, 1963 was the year Kim was buffeted by her own special storms. In a *Guideposts* writing contest (she came in second and won $500), she explained how she felt during the first of two personal storms.

On September 21, 1963, I was a new student at Wheaton Academy in Wheaton, Illinois, a private Christian high school, and after three discouraging weeks I didn't see how I could continue. I was living 160 miles from home and studying with the sighted, but without Braille textbooks. At the end of three weeks, my mother came to school to visit me.

After supper while sitting in my room, I told my mother something which I knew would disturb her. I wanted to leave school. "I've never gotten such low grades," I said. "I don't feel accepted here. Everyone is always so busy that I hate to ask them to read my assignments to me. If this is the 'seeing' world, you can have it! I want to quit."

Very, very firmly, Mother spoke some unforgettable words. "You've got to face the world. It will never be easy. God has brought you this far in your life. Don't you think He will keep on helping?"

After Mother told me I had to face the world and that it would never be easy, I realized I was at a point of no return. Desperately I prayed, "Father, if I can't turn back, give me strength to move forward. I've tried to make my own decisions, but failed. Take my life and guide me as You have in the past." At that moment a new confidence came over me.

Since then I've had other problems to face and decisions to make. But life has taken on new dimensions because I realize God alone controls my life. September 21, 1963, was the day my faith meant most to me because in recognizing my utter helplessness, I learned the importance of total dependence on God.

Kim didn't know it then, but God was preparing her for a harder test of her faith which would come several years later. In the meantime, she began to understand that trials were not all bad. Maturity and endurance came no other way. Through studies in Romans and other scriptures, Kim for the first time faced the reality of her blindness.

In our Bible classes at school I learned that God who had begun a good work in me would finish what He had started. Also I came to understand that everyone has some weakness or handicap. Mine was blindness.

After the first three weeks at Wheaton Academy I made up my mind I was going to make my life worth something even though

I was blind. Some of my new friends hinted that I would never be able to surmount the odds of my blindness. But I learned that God could do something with my limitation. He is glorified when we are weak.

These were good words and true. Yet they were easier to say than practice. Part of Kim's problem during those first weeks was pride and a fiery determination to prove her independence to herself and her friends.

When I first came to the Academy I felt I should be more independent and responsible for myself. I didn't know anybody and nobody knew me. I had heard competition was great and was designed to prepare students for college. But things turned out to be different than I expected.

One difference was the problem of eating. The dorm students ate at assigned seats for breakfast and supper. This was so attendance could be taken. But at lunch we had cafeteria lines. At the beginning this was difficult. I would wait a long time. I was too proud to ask for help.

The feeling of being "left out" was not, as Kim thought, a problem of nonacceptance. Rather, many new students and some staff members, sensing Kim's disorientation, felt embarrassed and hesitant to offer their help. It was a breakdown in communication—a lack of experience, sensitivity, and understanding of how to live and work with non-sighted people. Fortunately, this soon changed.

I learned I needed to be humble enough to ask for help. I never forgot this lesson and now when I truly need help, I'm not afraid to ask. It was good I found out the problem, because right after that things began to change.

One of the first things to change was her name. Up until now she had been Jeanie Kim Wickes. But since she happened to be rooming with three other girls, one of whom was a Jean, something had to happen.

"You don't look like a Jean to me," said her roommate one day. "You look more like a Kim. How about calling Jean, Jean, and you Kim?"

They agreed, it stuck, and Kim was happy to be Kim once again.

After word got out about Kim feeling down, her life at the Academy and later at Wheaton College was never quite the same. Her good friend Ginger Johnson, an attractive, dimple-cheeked member of the same choir team, recalled those early days.

"She wore sweaters and bobby socks and had her black hair curled around her head. She was cute. The first few days at school she seemed pretty scared. But as she became more relaxed, Kim turned into an independent dynamo.

"The Academy building was an old two-story former hospital with open staircases. But this didn't bother Kim. She seemed to know instinctively where these were. She'd barrel down the hall so fast we all had to watch out. We watched out because she carried a clipboard we nicknamed her poker. Several times she accidently hit me in the side.

"If you knew her, she liked to walk beside you, but she never took your arm. She walked with her arms by her side and would lightly touch your arm. It was the first time I had seen anyone so relaxed with their handicap. The fellows loved her and made sure she got to go to all the functions. And they loved to joke and tease. They would tell her that her slip was showing or ask when she was going to take Driver's Ed. One time the guys got her into their locker room. It was a riot! But they never did anything to make fun of her. They had great respect for her and, much to Kim's frustration, treated her like a sister.

"Kim always sat next to me in choir and would help and encourage me in my singing. She was always kind and happy when I got a solo part and was never upset if she didn't get a part. There wasn't one person I knew who, after getting to know her, felt sorry for her. And I don't remember her ever feeling sorry for herself.

"The more you were with her, the more you thought she had eyes. Sometimes I would forget she was blind and when I realized it again, it always surprised me. One day she leaned over and said, 'You're blond, aren't you?' We knew each other so well that it shocked me to hear her ask this. I laughed and said, 'No, I'm not blonde. I have brown hair and brown eyes.' I suppose she heard blondes have more fun because she said, 'You're not kidding me? I thought for sure you were blonde.'

"Sometimes I would walk her into her room at night and forget she couldn't see. 'For Pete's sake!' I'd say, 'Turn the lights on! How do you expect people to see in here with the lights off!' She always laughed.

"Kim was not always sweetness and light. She was never phony, but she could be stubborn. For reasons I could never understand at the time, Kim had an insatiable desire to be first academically. She lived in the dorm, where the rule was lights out at ten o'clock. They called it 'The Pumpkin Hour.' But Kim was never ready for bed by ten because she always had so much more to do than the rest of us. Along with her regular schoolwork at the Academy, she took correspondence courses in German and biology from Hadley School for the Blind in Winnetka, Illinois. She was their Student of the Year in 1964. Mayor Richard Daley presented her the award for 'outstanding scholastic achievement.'

"She often had to wait until someone could come and read her assignments. At other times she had to type her Braille notes, which were always huge. So to get everything completed, she often sat up long after the Pumpkin Hour. When she did and the supervisor found her sitting in the dark studying, she would say, 'Now, Kim. It's past ten o'clock. You must go to sleep.'

"A lot of other kids broke the rules and studied under the sheets with a flashlight and never got caught. But not Kim. The teachers always found her out. And even after they told her it was past time, she was stubborn enough to break the rules in order to get her work completed.

"I think this was the main reason she wasn't chosen to be on the National Honor Society even though she had a 3.9 average. It was a tragic blow for her which I think she carried through the rest of her schooling. I know it contributed greatly to her struggles with her Christian faith."

But breaking the rules of the Pumpkin Hour wasn't the only reason Kim didn't make the National Honor Society in her senior year at Wheaton Academy. Because she was unable to get physics texts in Braille and had to spend three hours each day trying to keep up, she decided to drop the course after the first semester. She also dropped band, a noncredit course she had taken as a fun subject. It gave her the extra time for her other subjects, but it also labeled her a "quitter" by one of the faculty.

"I understand your concern, Kim," said the Wheaton Academy headmaster, "but before I explain, I must ask your two friends to leave. . . . Now, Kim, you were considered for the Honor Society during your junior year, but there were too many other outstanding students and we thought you would have the opportunity during your senior year. However, because you dropped physics and band, Miss _____ concludes you to be a quitter.

"There is also the matter of the Pumpkin Hour rule. Some faculty members feel your persistent studying after 'lights out' sets a poor example for the freshman and junior students and is unbecoming

Kim: My Long Night

conduct for a senior student at Wheaton Academy. Also, more than once I've found you falling asleep during chapel. Kim, you're an outstanding student. But to be on the National Honor Society requires the recommendation of all the faculty. Since those who get elected do so by more than just scholarship, I have no alternative but to deny your request for reconsideration."

In later life Kim would confess that the Lord allowed this to happen to keep her from becoming too proud and to show her she must keep her eyes on Him, not people. She would also acknowledge that Jim Barnes was right when he said, "Sometimes the bitter experiences of life can be used by God to teach us important lessons." But at the time, all Kim acknowledged was her deep hurt, anger, and confusion.

> During the school year I spent most every weekend singing or
> speaking at some church. I have never quit anything I thought was
> important and I didn't think that course was important. I brought
> up my scholastic record, but it was useless. In the end I cried and
> began to question Christian people.

The bitter and crushing disappointment of not being elected to the Honor Society brought into focus a latent subconscious problem—ambivalent Christianity. She believed that openness, progress, an appreciation of the arts, excellence in learning, truth, kindness, and an honest concern for the needy were some of the attitudes and conduct professed by Christians. Yet here was a decision she considered grossly unfair. From out of the halls of her memory she began to chew over past events she felt incompatible with her faith and practice. Why were so many Christians occupied with trivia? It seemed their only interests were ball games, hairstyles, who was going with whom, and beauty pageants. All of a sudden Kim began to feel her world was different and she wanted out.

10. Don't Forget Your Flashlight

"What in the world will I do with a blind girl in the Adirondack Mountains?"

"Kim Wickes is an extraordinary 17–year–old," said Jim Barnes, "and I can assure you if you have her sing at your Friday and Saturday night concerts, Camp-of-the-Woods will never be the same. As far as mobility is concerned, Kim has an uncanny ability to quickly orient herself to her new environment.

"She's no stranger to camp life," continued Jim. "At fifteen she was chosen best camper (for handicapped children) at Camp Koch in southern Indiana. And she's no stranger to traveling. For graduation she and her high school graduating class took a chartered bus trip to Miami, and later she went on a concert tour to Colorado and Arizona. I think her coming to your camp would be a good lesson in faith—both on your part and Kim's."

"I don't understand," said the camp supervisor. "How would Kim's coming to sing at our concerts take faith if she gets paid for it?"

"First," said Jim, "the non-handicapped must learn that the so-called handicapped need to be given an opportunity to demonstrate that they can make it on their own. And conversely, when people like Kim go into a new experience, they need to exercise their faith and learn that the Lord can work things out for them."

"Speaking of faith," asked the supervisor, "how is hers?"

"Kim has great confidence in the Lord," said Jim. "However, just now she's having a little problem relating to Christian people. She needs to understand that Christians are not infallible—that they do make mistakes. She's in a period of questioning—not of her faith or of the Word of God, or even of her own commitment. Rather, she wonders, since her faith is untested, if it's strong enough for the 'real world.' I think a summer here at your camp will do wonders for Kim and bring her out of her shell."

Jim's fine reasoning did not totally convince the camp supervisor that Kim would work out, but with a good-natured sigh, he said, "Okay, we'll give her a chance."

It was late afternoon when Kim, along with Jim and his wife, arrived at Camp-of-the-Woods in Lake Pleasant, New York. Arrangements were made for Kim to sleep in the infirmary, which was next to the road and dining room and not too far into the woods. As those who came to welcome her to camp were about to leave, one woman turned to Jim and said, "You had better make sure she has her flashlight."

In all it was a delightful summer for Kim. She swam, sailed, and sang. After hearing her sing and watching the reaction and enthusiasm of the many people who came to the weekend concerts, the camp supervisor's former skepticism did a complete turnabout. He was so impressed that he asked Kim to return the following summer.

In the fall of 1965, Kim again went back to school, this time to Wheaton College, a private Christian liberal arts college with an outstanding academic reputation. One of her teachers, Ellen Thompson, chairman of the Conservatory's piano theory department, recalls what it was like to teach Kim.

"When Kim applied to Wheaton I was asked if I could work out the details for a blind student. I said I would. I delight in having a challenge! At first I thought it would be rather difficult, but it turned out just the opposite. Kim was an exceptional student—apt and cheerful—and learning seemed to be almost effortless. It was as if all I needed to do was make a suggestion, then stand aside and watch her grow. Having her for my student was a great learning experience for me.

"It still baffles me when I think how she scooted around the halls quicker than any of us, and stopped right on the brink of the stairwells!"

Like many of Kim's friends, Ellen frequently forgot that Kim didn't understand nonverbal body language and the nuances of the aging process which sighted people take for granted.

"It surprised me one day when we were talking about what people looked like and how they change as they get older," said Ellen. 'Can you tell in a young child what he's going to look like when he gets older?' she asked. I had never been asked that question before and I was hard put to explain the changes that take place between childhood and adulthood.

"Kim's basic musicianship came out of her singing. She had such remarkable intuitive powers and natural feeling of expression that accompanying her when she sang was pure joy. One day she accidentally gave me an insight into how difficult it is for a blind person to read music. I was following along in my score while she played, and I noticed a note different from what I had on my score. It wasn't a wrong note as far as she was concerned. She had just learned it that way. I stopped her and asked if she had a different note at that point. I thought that since the music was in Braille, she would be able to feel it in the music, values, and relationships. But she began to read: 'In the first measure of the right hand, treble clef, note on the third line is flattened for two beats.'

"I was dumbfounded! Her music was all written out in Braille.

All those words just to give one note on the staff!

"Kim and I had a warm relationship during her year at Wheaton. I wish she could have remained with us but she was accepted, through the Hadley School for the Blind, as an exchange student to Germany. She wanted to study German and voice in Europe. However, at the last moment this fell through and she transferred to Indiana University. She wanted to take advantage of their excellent music department.

"Just before Kim, left I knew she was a little disillusioned in her Christian life, trying to sort things out in her own mind. I knew also it was hard for her to get into the Word as she should. It was always a problem to find someone to read to her. I told her that whenever she felt like talking to someone to call me, no matter what part of the country she was in. She seemed to have so many struggles that I wanted to encourage her."

While Kim's struggles with how she thought Christians should live their lives fomented toward the end of her year at Wheaton, during her second summer at Camp-of-the-Woods in 1966 they exploded.

I knew Christianity was right, but it bothered me to find so much cynicism among some of the Christian students at Wheaton. One day I walked from my dorm to the music building. There were some twists in the sidewalk and I was being careful to follow them. As I was about to get off the sidewalk, some boys clapped and made funny noises. It confused me and I had to struggle to find my way. This was not typical of all the kids, but it added to my disillusionment.

Cynicism directed toward other people upset me, too. Once on a gospel tour we passed a man on the road with a flag directing traffic. Someone said, "It sure must take a lot of brains to do that."

But what upset me most was complacency. It hit me hard one day during the summer after we had heard a speaker from Wycliffe Bible Translators. I didn't know what this organization did before and was impressed that they were trained linguists. I know how important it is to communicate with people in their own language. I started to talk to a boy and told him how impressed I was with Wycliffe and the work they were doing with the minority groups around the world. But all the boy said was, "Ask me if I care."

Once again I thought, "I'm in a place where I don't belong." I was confused. I didn't fit in with this kind of person. At Wheaton Academy the teachers told us that if we had been given a lot then a lot was required of us, that Christians had the responsibility of sharing the gospel and the good things we learn about Jesus Christ with everybody.

After transferring to Indiana University at Bloomington, Kim began a spiritual odyssey that was to last almost eight years. As in her previous school careers, her most important and immediate problem was orientation to her new surroundings. And as before, she met the challenge head-on. In a letter to her mother after her first week, she wrote, "I walked down the hall tonight and introduced myself and got acquainted with all my neighbors."

"Later when I visited her," said Eva, "I found myself getting lost. But not Jeanie. She knew her way around the campus as if she was guided by radar. And in her own building it wasn't any time before she could run up the stairs, punch the bell for the elevator, get in by herself, push the button for the floor she needed, get off, then run down the hall, stop right in front of her door, and bolt through her door just as if she could see."

It was true she couldn't see, but it wasn't for lack of trying and praying. At Wheaton College a friend began telling her it wasn't God's will for her to be blind and encouraged her to pray to God to return her sight.

The same thing happened at Indiana University, except that this time a group of her new friends persuaded her to attend special healing services in Pittsburgh. Carefully, Eva cautioned Kim about what might *not* happen.

"Just remember, Jeanie," she said, "if you don't get healed, God is just the same. He still loves you. Don't let a disappointment turn you away."

It turned out to be a long, hard trip with predictable results. Several years later Kim spoke of these two events.

> I prayed and prayed every day and nothing happened. It was the same at the healing service in Pittsburgh. In reflection I know I should have prayed for a deeper understanding of the way God works. I should have asked for His grace to help me accept what He allowed to be taken away.

Kim began her studies at Indiana University with the same vigor and discipline she always brought to her schooling. At first she also maintained her Christian testimony and willingly fought for Christian principles. One particular group she bandied words with was a group of Jewish girls. They thought Kim was the first smart Christian they had ever met. But as the months wore on, Kim's attitude changed.

> It seemed to me the music programs of the churches I attended were poor. If the sermon was good, the choir was bad, or if the choir was good, the sermon was bad. Gradually I became disinterested in church and Christianity. I stopped reading the Bible and stopped praying.
>
> In the spring of 1967, my mother was chosen Mother of the Year for Indiana. I went home, unwillingly, to take part in the ceremony. I was a little frustrated because of an important exam I had to take and I didn't want to take the time away from studying.

When I came home, Mom asked me to sing her favorite song, "His Eye Is on the Sparrow." I didn't want anything to do with it. I thought it was inferior music, but I sang it anyway. Afterward I thought that if Christianity means having that kind of taste, forget it!

Kim now admits that her junior year at I.U. was a year of grave doubts and confusion. Her parents were concerned over her disinterest in spiritual matters and the unhealthy effects of a secular college. On the other hand, Kim was upset because she thought her parents were not supportive of her choice of career as a concert soloist. She didn't understand why they, and her friend Ginger, were uneasy over this choice. "All they could see was the problem of who would go with me and take me around. But this was the least of my worries."

By her senior year, Kim's spiritual life began a slow but steady turn for the better. The first indication of change was her acceptance of an invitation to join Inter-Varsity Christian Fellowship. Committed to thoughtful and penetrating exploration of God's Word and the strengthening and up-building of the Christian student's spiritual life, Inter-Varsity's stimulus was exactly what Kim needed.

Inter-Varsity had their meetings every Friday night. I liked the things they said. I knew they had to be smart. Their president was Martin Price, a Ph.D. in chemistry.

Through reading many of the good Inter-Varsity books, especially Francis Schaeffer's, my attitude began to change. (I met Dr. Schaeffer and his wife when he spoke at Wheaton College. They invited me to visit them at L'Abri in the Swiss Alps.)

As I read, I talked with the Inter-Varsity staffers, and thought about what was happening in my life, I began to realize that my rebellion was not against Jesus Christ. It was against a religious system which I felt did not meet my needs.

During my Wheaton days and my early days at I.U., I assumed that Jesus communicated the same light to all His children. He doesn't. It finally hit me that God is a God of diversity and infinite variety. Just look at the flowers, animals, and people!

I began to understand that God didn't create every person the same. Each has different gifts, talents, and tastes. Suddenly I saw how deeply wrong it was of me to want everyone to enjoy a Gregorian chant or a Bach fugue or the works of Handel, Mozart, Haydn, or Beethoven—or even a barbershop quartet!

I began to see that there could be unity in diversity and that God wants His children to use and develop their God-given talents and gifts. I decided then to be a different Christian than I had been and resolved not to be mediocre.

Kim was as good as her intentions. She began a regular time of personal devotions and actively sought out the fellowship of Christians. When she heard that Francis Schaeffer was again speaking at Wheaton College, she bussed from Bloomington to Wheaton by herself in spite of the heavy load of nineteen hours she was taking.

It was refreshing to hear Dr. Schaeffer affirm the truth of Christianity and stress the absolutes of Scripture. Among many of my non-Christian friends, this concept was old-fashioned. They all talked about relevancy. But I said amen to absolutes!

Kim meant what she said and began to live out these concepts. But she had not yet reckoned with her womanhood.

11. No Place to Put the Fire

The full-page article appeared in the July 5, 1969, issue of the Lafayette, Indiana, *Journal and Courier*. In a few short paragraphs the writer skipped through Kim's years in America. Those who remembered what she had been like when she first arrived on that cold November in 1957 shook their heads in amazement at what this tiny blind Korean girl had accomplished in twelve short years. And as they read about her future, they were further amazed.

Jean Kim Wickes, a 22–year–old Korean-born woman, has graduated with high distinction on June 9 with a Bachelor of Music from the Indiana University School of Music. She will spend the summer in Europe attending conferences and touring. . . .

Majoring in voice with a minor in piano, Jean became a member of Mu Phi Epsilon and Pi Kappa Lambda professional sorority at I.U. She was distinguished by attaining the highest scholastic average for the college chapter. She graduated with a 3.88 out of a possible 4.0

"I've always been interested in music," said the petite graduate, who has perfect pitch. "I plan to go for my master's degree in September. It's a two-year program and that will give me time to decide what to do when I'm done. . . ."

To learn a musical selection written in Braille, Jean must first feel the Braille with her left hand to find out and play the right hand's portion. Then the process is reversed and she plays with her left hand. . . .

She never used a Seeing Eye dog because she has never had enough time to attend the then six-week training course needed to acquire a dog.

"I've always had too many things to do that I never had six weeks all together," explained Jean, who was the only undergraduate blind student at I.U.

The biggest problem Jean encountered at school was finding suitable people to read to her. This did not come up very often. She said most people were willing to help her. . . .

"Sometimes," added Jean, "it's hard on a teacher who has never had a blind student before and you feel you have to prove yourself to this teacher. But after a while it works out okay."

When it came to test taking, Jean would have someone ask her the questions orally. She would then type out the answers on a standard typewriter or dictate her answers to her teacher. She prefers the oral tests "because it's quicker."

During her two-month European tour Jean will attend a month-long conference at Schloss Mittersill in Austria (a refurbished castle) sponsored by the International Fellowship of Evangelical Students. . . . Later she will leave for L'Abri, Switzerland.

Language will not be a problem for the active young lady. She speaks German and has a working knowledge of French and Italian. Her English is excellent, though she still does her arithmetic in Korean.

"I think they might be surprised when I speak to them in German, considering I'm Korean and an American citizen [she was sworn in at the Lafayette courthouse in June 1960]," she said confidently. "It should be an enjoyable trip."

"How can anything happen to me?" said Kim to her mother. "It's an Indiana University charter flight direct from Indianapolis to London to Paris and back home again. Besides, my friend Emily and her brother will be with me."

"Yes," said Eva, "but they will be with you only as far as London. I don't think it's good for a blind person, or a girl, to be traveling alone all over Europe."

By her own admission Eva is a mother who likes to have her children close by her side. And her objection to Kim's proposed European trip was typical of most protective mothers. Yet Eva knew from experience that when Kim set her mind on an idea or project, almost nothing on earth could dissolve the intensity of her desire.

> I wanted to go to Europe for a change of pace. I was tired of studying and practicing all the time. I was in a mood to be silly. Besides, I wanted to see as much of the world as I could. Also, Martin Price, president of Inter-Varsity at I.U., told me about the conference at Schloss Mittersill and I wanted to go.
>
> I had my own money from singing at weddings and a little saved from my allowance. I just knew it would be fun, and in spite of my parents' fears I went. But when we first landed in London at midnight I wasn't so sure it was going to be fun.
>
> Suddenly it hit me that I was on a new continent far from home, and I was a little scared.

Kim's fears, however, soon vanished in a happy round of exciting adventures and a new sense of freedom.

> My friend Emily was not a Christian but she was thoughtful and bright and seemed to sense my needs before I asked. It was a happy five days in London. We stayed up late, ate at an Indian restaurant,

had fish and chips in Piccadilly, and I listened while Emily explained all the important sights. We had a ball!

At the end of the five days, I told Emily I must go to Cologne, Germany. There was a big Braille library there and I wanted to see what was available in German Braille. She helped me get to the American Express office and we separated.

I explained to the American Express people that I wanted a hotel near the library, not too expensive. And I went all by myself, flying from London to Cologne. This was the first time I had ever done anything as big as this. It was exciting but a little frightening to be alone. When I arrived in Cologne, American Express was there. They took me to my hotel.

The following morning Kim called a taxi and visited the Cologne Cathedral. As in London, she used her fingers to sightsee.

I patted the floor, talked to the guard, and felt the texture and shape of the statues with the tips of my fingers. They were beautiful. It was wonderful to see all those things and I felt free, oh so free.

Making all her own arrangements, Kim flew from Cologne to Munich. In Munich she bussed to the train station and, with the help of a Red Cross attendant, took the train to Inter-Varsity's International Conference at Schloss Mittersill.

Those who travel know there will be at least one element of surprise to confound the prearranged plans of the most astute journeyer. Kim had two.

Her first surprise was the language. Kim spoke German but found she couldn't communicate with the southern Germans, who spoke the Bavarian dialect.

They all sounded like they had mashed potatoes in their mouths. I spent a few hours of uncertainty in Munich when I tried to get the Red Cross station attendant to understand what I wanted, but in the end it all worked out. The people were nice and gave me bread and cheese to eat. When the agent put me on the right train to reach Schloss Mittersill, she expressed amazement that a blind girl who couldn't speak the Bavarian dialect should be traveling alone. If I could have communicated clearly and thought about it immediately, I would have told her I never travel alone. Jesus Christ is always with me—always!

Conceived by Inter-Varsity's Stacey Woods as a Christian student training center and conference retreat, Schloss Mittersill was all that Kim imagined.

As soon as I opened the door it smelled like a castle, or how you think a castle should smell! There was the aroma of good European soup and fresh-baked bread and the smell of Bavarian sausage.

Because it was high in the mountains, outside I could smell the wild summer flowers, the sun was warm and friendly, and it felt good to be alive.

Indeed it was good to be alive—until Kim met surprise number two. Then she wasn't so sure!

I was on the sun deck when a bee crawling between the cracks in the boards stung my foot. If that wasn't bad enough, the next day a hornet stung the instep of the same foot when I went on a little hike. My foot swelled and the doctor made me stay in bed. It reminded me a little of when I once used poison ivy leaves as TP on a camping trip. I swelled so bad I couldn't move. Now here I was again having to crawl inch by inch to the bathroom.

After a while the boys carried me to the lectures. It was funny. There I was singing Mozart's "Allelujah" in the sitting position and my foot stuck out in front of me resting on a chair with a fat pillow under it. But that was all right, too, because I met many more students, and I liked that.

They came from all over Europe. Some even came from behind the Iron Curtain. They were intelligent and asked smart, insightful questions during Bible studies and lecture times. Most of the students had traveled and broadened their interests above staying home and accumulating material goods. There was also a great feeling of love for the body of Christ. Hardly anyone ever argued.

I was impressed and took notes all day long with my stylus. After four weeks, when the conference ended, I had gained many new friends plus a new insight about the gospel. I understood more clearly that the gospel wasn't just in America. This inspired me. I wanted to return to grad school at I.U. and turn the campus upside-down for Jesus.

If Kim's spiritual batteries were recharged at Schloss Mittersill, they became overcharged at L'Abri. Designed and dedicated to the Christian's spiritual growth, L'Abri (which means "shelter" in French) is an idyllic community of fourteen picture-postcard chalets. It's a place which fosters meaningful relations—with Christ through prayer and Bible study, and with those who live and visit there.

"L'Abri," said Edith, wife of founder Francis Schaeffer, "is a place where we strive to make love real among us and not simply to have it as a slogan."

At the end of her blissful, happy summer, Kim returned to Dayton and then to I.U. to work on her master's degree. She received this in September 1971, and would later work toward her doctorate. The spiritual efflorescence of Kim's time at L'Abri and Schloss Mittersill was still fresh in her mind, and she was anxious to share everything she had learned and experienced with her friends. But her enthusiasm was to evaporate like dew before a hot summer's sun.

I didn't want it to. I fought hard against it, but when I got back to the Midwest I felt boxed in. The people I was meeting hadn't traveled much and they had their own interests and friends.

Two undergraduate Christian girls asked me to be their suite mate, and I lived in the undergraduate dorm with them. They were great! They picked me up and helped me all they could, but our fellowship times were different than what I had come to love in Europe. There was little deep intellectual probing. I felt helpless— like falling into a deep valley after a mountaintop experience. I was all fired up, but there was no place to put the fire. And then I met Charles.

His major was organ, and he was a musical genius—very talented, very witty, very tall! I barely came up to his shoulder. Besides being with him at the music department at I.U., he played the organ at the same church where I sang each Sunday.

I had written my Jewish friends and tried to share some of the things I learned at L'Abri. They wrote back and told me I would soon get over my enthusiasm. They challenged my statement that Jesus Christ is the only way to know God. Then after I got to know Charles better, I tried to talk to him about the Lord.

"You're too smart to believe the Bible," he said. I was crushed and confused. He was so smart that I loved being with him. When we talked about music or played the instruments or joked, we flowed together like a symphony. I would have to say I was in love. I had not met any Christian males who were as talented in the arts as Charles. Also, he seemed so efficient when he took me out. But sometimes he could be nasty and thoughtless. He would take me to a concert and sometimes just leave me there if he saw someone else. Later, when I told him I thought it was stupid of him to leave me there, he would say, "It never occurred to me it was stupid." When that happened, I used to wonder if a Christian boy would have acted that way.

The years from 1970 to the fall of 1973 were for Kim—and the world—a kaleidoscope of excitement and problems without historical precedent. Intermingled with wondering about the outcome of the Chicago Seven conspiracy trial and biting her fingernails over the near-disaster of Apollo 13, Kim tried to cope with her own personal disasters.

First, in May 1971 she received word from the Indiana Agency for the Blind that they could no longer continue her financial aid (they had helped her for two years during her master's program). "We must concentrate on the undergraduates who need our help," they said. Charles, who loomed as her biggest disaster, did not encourage her to apply for a teaching assistantship. "It's an advantage to be blind," he said. "Don't worry about the money. The agency will come through."

But the agency didn't come through and she did worry. In addition, she was getting some typical parental pressure. "Don't you think it's about time you got out and got a job?" became a frequent subject in letters and home visits.

Kim was too proud to share her problems and depression with Charles. Instead, she chose (as she always did in the crunch) to share her problems with her Christian friends. This time it was Ken and Linda, an engaged couple she met when she first came to I.U. In a torrent of bewilderment and the first hint of self-pity anyone had ever seen in Kim, she poured out her heart.

"Nobody needs me," she told Ken and Linda. "I don't have money to pay for my education next year, and if I don't spend time getting my education, what is there for me to do? I now understand why people feel there is no reason to live; why they want to kill themselves. I might as well alleviate the problem of overpopulation, too."

Then with wet, wet tears Kim told Ken and Linda how scared she was about getting a job like her parents wanted her to. She confessed her frustration over Charles. She knew he wasn't good for her, but found him "so attractive. The heart has reasons the mind knows nothing about," she said. "I tried to tell him about my problems, but couldn't bring myself to do it. All he did was leave mad, slamming the door!"

"Oh, Kim," said Ken, "we've been praying for you, hoping we could help you. You've lived a pretty wild life since meeting Charles. I've noticed you don't talk about the Lord as much as you used to. Your interest in spiritual things is not what it was a few years ago.

"Part of the problem is that when we Christians have a great spiritual high like you did at L'Abri, Satan immediately comes in and tries to destroy the memory of that fellowship. He tempts us all the harder. Remember, Jesus was tempted right after His baptism. There are examples all through the Bible of people who had a great spiritual experience, and then Satan tried to rob them of their joy right after their victory. The Bible says that if we draw near to God, He will draw near to us, and the devil flees. But the fight is never easy. Kim, don't you think it's about time you draw near to the Lord again, and start going to church and reading the Scriptures again?"

"Yes," said Kim, "I do."

And she did. Yet she still held strong feelings for Charles. Moreover, his agnosticism shifted her spiritual focus. She began her old habit of scrutinizing people's mental agility. If it didn't measure up to hers and Charles', she criticized them (most often inwardly) for being dull. She didn't want to be associated with a dull Christianity.

But then there occurred several other "disasters" which she would say later "taught me that when God loves His children, He chastens to teach them things He wants them to learn. And when the chips are down, it is Christians who always come through."

In December 1971 Kim spent several days visiting her sister Mary Lou, who was now married and living in Wilmington, Delaware. On the day she was to leave, Kim displayed her chronic independence and attempted to lift her heavy suitcase off the counter in the bathroom. (Kim still packs a big red suitcase which most men struggle to lift!)

I picked up the fat suitcase, but it unexpectedly fell off, jerking down and carrying me sideways. The pain was bad. When I got to New York I couldn't walk. The doctor told me it was a muscle spasm. It wasn't. I found out later it was a slipped disc. On top of that I developed a fever and a horrible ache in my side. When I arrived back in Indianapolis, I was taken off the plane in a wheelchair. I felt terrible. I was always a limber girl. And when Charles met me, I was humiliated. They took me right to the hospital.

After a series of tests, Kim was moved from the Bloomington Hospital to Indiana University Medical Center, where she underwent further testing. Her fever and side ache were diagnosed as a kidney infection. She promptly spent the next three weeks in bed alternating between traction, heat therapy for her back, and special medication for the infection.

Kim missed the first half of her 1972 winter semester and was alarmed about missing her studies. But being apart by herself was just what God wanted. From her hospital bed Kim learned some infinitely valuable and lifelong lessons.

During my time in the hospital I found I had a great many Christian

friends. Some phoned almost every day and read me Bible verses.
A couple called and said God was chastening me. I believed them.
I thought this was God's judgment for not being as close to Him as
I should have been. Now I don't know if that was right or wrong,
but I do know I began to understand that God wanted me to start
thinking seriously about how I was spending my life. It became clear
to me that what was happening was for my own good. It was the
first time in years that I had stopped long enough from my studies
and trying to have fun to listen to God.

In the hospital and later in my dorm when I was recuperating, all kinds of visitors came to see me. Three special people who
came were pastors from three different denominational churches.
One was Pastor Ferris from the Bloomington United Presbyterian
Church. He told me his church was praying for me. This encouraged
me, and for a while when I was in so much pain and couldn't feed
myself he, along with the other pastors, fed me if they happened
to come at mealtimes.

Once a missionary couple bought me a cassette booklet with the
whole New Testament on it. I began to understand I didn't know the
Scriptures as well as I thought I did. It was a hard, painful time, but I
learned that love and not intelligence is the most important element
for a Christian to display. And when it comes to the nitty gritty, it's
Christian people who really care and take time out to help.

Besides visitors, Kim received a great many cards and letters. Two
of the letters she received, however, did not express concern for her
health.

The first came in early January and was postmarked Chonan,
Korea—her hometown. It was from her Korean father!

In 1970 the Holt Adoption Agency gave Kim's name and address
to a Korean newspaper reporter doing a series of follow-up stories on

Korean war orphans. After visiting the Wickes in Dayton and hearing Kim's story, the reporter wrote a special feature on Kim which appeared in the *Korea Times,* Korea's largest newspaper. Always looking for the drama in a story, the reporter highlighted the river incident. It was this which caught the attention of Kim's father. He knew it was indeed his daughter, and he wrote her.

> God has always supplied my need when I have needed it. When I received my father's letter I couldn't read it. But there were some Korean music students at I.U. who could. This in part is what they read to me as I lay in the hospital bed: "Little Eun Jooni, at night when I look into the stars I miss you and I cry. I am not well. I have been in the hospital. Could you please come to visit me? Your Father."

Kim's second letter came after she left the hospital and was recuperating in her dorm. This letter had a New York postmark and was written in English. It was from the Fulbright Commission and informed her that she had been rejected for the Fulbright Scholarship for study in Vienna, Austria, at the Vienna Institute of Music. But rejection is never final for Kim. She applied again a year later and was accepted.

For Kim this was the *summum bonum* of all her achievements, the fulfillment of all she had dreamed of since her trombone-playing adoptive grandfather and Al Stewart first began encouraging her to reach for the stars. But Kim's ecstasy was to be short-lived. There's nothing quite so disillusioning as believing you've arrived!

12. God Never Works Too Early

"The Optacon Converter is a great little reading machine," said the counselor at the Indiana Agency for the Blind. "As you draw the small optical scanner across a printed page, it picks up each ink print letter and translates it into tiny, needle-like protrusions which you feel and read with your index finger."

"However, Kim, the Optacon is expensive—like $5,000—and it takes a great deal of skill to learn how to read and handle the machine. Not every blind person can. There's also a waiting list because they're handmade in Palo Alto, California. If you have to get one by August 17, my advice is to forget it. There's no way you could possibly get one in three weeks even if you had the money. Why don't you wait until you get back from Vienna and then look into it?"

The counselor didn't know it, but telling Kim she can't do something is like attempting to stop a wild herd of buffalo.

Early in June 1973 Kim learned through the Fulbright Commission that there would be no possibility of getting extra monies to pay readers, even if they could be found. This meant that an independent reading source was imperative if Kim was to complete her studies in Vienna. What happened between July 21 and August 17 is nothing short of a modern-day miracle.

I had heard of the Optacon reading machine but dismissed the idea

of ever getting one because of the expense. Now that there would
not be readers available in Europe, it was a must.

I wrote to Stanford University, where the Optacon is made,
and told them about myself, the Fulbright Scholarship, and why I
needed an Optacon. I also told them I needed to know before the
end of summer school on August 17, since I was leaving for Vienna
on September 20. I prayed and asked the Lord to indicate by their
response what I should do.

Seven days later, on July 21, I received a long-distance phone
call. It was a Tuesday night and ordinarily I would have been out
practicing. Also, I now had a private room with phone. It was often
frustrating because when I was out there was no one to receive my
calls. But the Lord was working. He sent rain that Tuesday night
and kept my by the phone.

"Hello," said a voice. "This is Paul Obester from Stanford. I
am calling about your inquiry into the Optacon. First let me say
we were all deeply impressed with your letter. Next, we have two
machines already made, so availability is not a problem. Third, we
conduct the ten-day training classes only once a month. There's one
coming up in August, which will conflict with your summer school
program, and the next one will be too late for you. However, we've
decided to give you a special training program if you can make it
out here before you leave."

I told him I didn't know what to say except that I would come
for the training session. I explained I didn't have a penny. I was getting a small amount from a teaching assistantship and had a little
loan to pay back. Yet I knew I had to have that reading machine.
When I hung up I began praying and writing letters.

Kim says the next three weeks were the busiest she has ever known.
Between writing all the service clubs she could think of (thirty in all,

including Colonel Sanders), she packed four years' accumulated possessions, planned shipping arrangements, wrote her summer finals, and practiced two or three hours a day for a benefit concert.

I only got about three hours' sleep each night, and the last week of school I wore the same dress every day. But it was amazing, exciting, and scary to see God work. A lot of my friends said later my energy and faith that God was going to supply was an inspiration to them.

But as the days passed and I didn't hear from any of the service clubs, I began to worry a bit. Eli Lilly, where my dad had worked for twenty-five years, said they would like to help buy the machine but could only help through special organized foundations and projects, not individuals.

Then a friend, Kay Kersey, suggested that I write Mr. Sarkes Tarzian, a wealthy Bloomington businessman. A lot of people in Bloomington said he was a tightwad. But that didn't matter to me. I thought, "nothing ventured, nothing gained," and I wrote.

I tried to get in to see Dean Webb at I.U. to endorse my letter or write a letter to Mr. Tarzian, telling him not to overlook my letter. I figured Mr. Tarzian would get a bunch of letters and I didn't want my letter sitting on his desk after August 17.

"I'm sorry, Kim," said Dean Webb's secretary. "He's working on a new budget and the earliest you can see him is next week on the thirteenth." That was the last Monday of summer school, but I waited.

"This is a worthy project, Kim," said the dean after he looked at my picture of the Optacon, "but I can't get involved in an individual project. Something like this must go through the Indiana University Foundation." I told him I didn't have time. Then he read my letter again and asked me what I wanted him to do. (I had known him a long time, though not as dean. He had been the choir director and had just become dean in May.) I told him I thought he should endorse my letter to Mr. Tarzian, that this was a special case, and that no one could hurt him for doing this. He said, "Okay."

After the dean endorsed the letter, I mailed it right away so it could get out in the five p.m. mail. Also, Kay Kersey arranged for the Morgan County *Gazette* to do a feature article on me. It just so happened that Mr. Tarzian owned the *Gazette!*

On Wednesday, August 15, I telephoned Mr. Tarzian to see if he had received a letter from Kim Wickes. He said, "Not yet," and asked when I had mailed it. I told him Monday. He said it sometimes takes seven days for a letter to cross town. I then told him to take a look at his evening *Gazette.*

I don't know if he ever looked at the *Gazette,* but on Thursday, August 16, I got a call from Dean Webb's office saying that Mr. Tarzian had phoned and I was to call back at four o'clock. I did but his secretary told me he was at the airport and would call me when he got back.

At last Mr. Tarzian did call. He talked slowly and calmly and sounded tall and competent. He told me he had received my letter and investigated to see if indeed there was such a machine. "I discovered there is," he said. "I'm going to buy it for you. I'm placing the order tomorrow."

I just couldn't believe it. I told him I had given a concert on the twelfth and was giving another on the nineteenth and had about $700 that I could contribute toward it. "No," he said, "you use that money for traveling to California for your special lessons."

When he hung up I fell back on my bed and felt my watch. It was midnight, August 16! In that instant I learned that God never works too early. He wants us to learn patience and trust and to know that He is going to supply in ways and means that are new and un-

expected. The reason? So *He* can be glorified, not man.

Later, when I called Mr. Tarzian from California, I said, "What can I do to thank you?"

"Don't do anything," he said. "Just use the machine."

When I told him he was an answer to prayer, he said, "That's what I want to be."

Encased in a bubble of excitement and spiritual euphoria, Kim bade farewell to her parents (who did not share her enthusiasm) as well as her friends at I.U. and left on schedule for Vienna.

Vienna! Vienna! City of gaiety, queen of the Danube! Its very name stirs the imagination—the monocle, the polite bow and simultaneous click of ebony heels, the hand placed firmly at the small of the waist, the petticoats and crinolines swishing and swirling to the heady triple rhythm of a Strauss waltz.

Under the Hapsburgs in the 1800s and 1900s this was indeed one of the faces of Vienna. It was the city which gave birth to the word *gemütlichkeit*—enjoyment of the good things of life—friendship, music, dining, and dancing. People like Haydn, Mozart, Beethoven, Schubert, Brahms, and Strauss, along with Sigmund Freud, Gustav Mahler, and many other notables, walked the narrow streets, sat in the coffeehouses, and created the legend of gloriously glamorous Vienna.

But when Kim arrived in September of 1973, she found that the Blue Danube was neither blue nor (by the time it reached Vienna) particularly beautiful. The once-smiling city was to Kim sad, dirty, smelly, and melancholy.

I had a friend named Heidi who worked for Operation Mobilization in Vienna. It was she who helped me get settled and oriented when I first arrived. She showed me how to wear a triangular armband which meant I was handicapped. If you wore it with the two dots going up it meant you were blind—or was it deaf? If you wore the dots going down, it meant the other handicap. We were never sure which was which! Heidi told me I wasn't under any circumstance to cross the street alone. "A blind woman was hit by a car the other day," she said, "and died on the way to the hospital. I don't think the people here are as concerned about blind persons."

I believed her. When I tried to get on and off the trains, people pushed and shoved through the same door trying to get on and off. Once, when I was with a friend, the train door snapped closed on my arm. They were not automatic and for a split second I had visions of being dragged along by the train. I screamed and the people screamed and the door opened. I wasn't hurt but my arm was sore for a few days. The conductor told me never to scream again.

When the tourist ads describe Vienna's inner city, they almost always mention the Ringstrasse, or inner boulevard, as a splendid example of Austrian architecture and statuary. Kim, however, did not empathize with the ad writers.

My dorm was right in the middle of the Ringstrasse. It was an old convent. It still had statues, stained glass windows, echoey hallways, and big open staircases that had no logic to them. In America there is usually a pattern to buildings, but not in Vienna.

We had a decrepit elevator which was so old I needed a key to use it. The elevator was only for the use of the girls who lived on the third and fourth floors. The boys were on the first two floors and did not use the elevator. But most of the time the elevator didn't work and I had to walk up to my room, which was at the end of the hall farthest from the elevator.

Almost immediately I felt lonely—so far away from anything I could call home. I felt separated, like no one knew what was happening to me. The Fulbright people were nice, but after the first five days of orientation I was on my own. In the dorm I kept wondering when all the students would assemble for a get-acquainted meeting, but it never happened. The only place students met was in the TV room. This was right across the hall from my room, but there was never any communication. Everyone just sat and smoked without talking. It was like being in a hotel. There was a small dining room, but the food was heavy, greasy, and starchy. Mostly I ate yogurt in my room—alone.

Without realizing what was happening, Kim allowed what she believed was the dreary gloominess of Vienna to enter into her being. There was an unexplainable emptiness which made her stomach feel hollow and which stuck in her throat like a cold chunk of unchewed mutton.

Except for a couple of American music friends and a few Evangelical Alliance missionaries whom she met on the weekends, and occasionally at prayer meetings, Kim was alone, totally without the support of social interaction. The result was culture shock. All during her school career and especially during her four years at I.U., Kim was never out of earshot of her friends. But not in Vienna. And if not knowing how to handle this new and unexplainable anxiety baffled her, she was dumbfounded by the way her classes were conducted.

No one seemed to know where classes were being held. Nothing was organized. Finally someone told me the classes were in an old building over a mile away from the dorm. I found it after great difficulty and going across many streets. For the first time in many years I used my cane. I had to. There were always cars parked on the sidewalk and other obstacles in the least expected places.

When I went to get the train I always prayed that the right people would be there to help me. But as frustrating as the obstacles were, none was quite as frustrating as trying to find where and when my next class was going to be held. Sometimes I would go and there would be a notice on the bulletin board saying that the teacher had called and canceled the class. At other times I sat for an hour and a half or even longer, waiting for a teacher. Sometimes they came; other times they didn't.

In addition to being upset by a loosely organized academic structure, Kim was even more upset by the loose moral environment. Yet it was this problem which helped her decide that she did not, after all, want to become a secular concert singer.

I thought my Fulbright study in Vienna was going to be a springboard into lieder or oratorio, or perhaps some other kind of secular career in the music world. But during my year in Vienna I began to lose interest in becoming famous and making a big name for myself. There were several reasons for this. For one, I had more time to read the Scriptures (with my new Optacon) and to pray.

I prayed about everything, almost constantly, because my thoughts were always on the Lord. In America I was always busy and under so much pressure that even when I wanted to have devotions I found them a chore. Not in Vienna! I looked forward to praying, and sometimes I sat for a whole hour in the tub just having sweet fellowship with the Lord.

I guess because I was enjoying the Lord in a new way I found the low moral standards and underhanded professional politics distasteful. I had seen a little of this at I.U.—fellows sleeping with their girls. But here it seemed sickening. I had also heard rumors about the "audition couch," but now it was all around me and part of my daily life—singers sleeping with the right conductors in order to get auditions and top placements. This was disillusioning to me. I knew I didn't want to be involved in this to get a job. I began to wonder if I had done the right thing by coming to Vienna.

I prayed and told the Lord that if I had done the wrong thing by majoring in music to somehow fix it up.

And God did "fix it up." He knew what Kim didn't—that conflict creates character, that only through hardship and testing come the finest wines. If Vienna was indeed a time of great testing, it was also a time of great opportunity and blessing.

Through one of Kim's music friends she was introduced to Frau Ludwig, then the 75–year–old mother of Christa, one of Metropolitan Opera's outstanding singers.

My friend Linda told me that the chance of Frau Ludwig taking me was one in a hundred, since she was old and no longer interested in taking students. But I went to see her in the country. It meant an hour by train and then a half-hour's walk. Also, I knew she charged about $35 to $40 an hour. I didn't know how I would pay for this, as my scholarship didn't provide money for private lessons. Also, if I paid that amount I didn't know how I was going to keep up my pledge to the Lord. (I had just decided to give a little gift each month to Christian work.)

Then I met Frau Ludwig. She liked me and took me as her student, and when I offered to pay her she said, "No, I am happy to give you free lessons." This teacher was one of the greatest musical blessings of my life!

I was overwhelmed. To think I was being taught by the most

coveted voice teacher in Europe! This showed me God always gives you more than you think you are giving Him.

It was Frau Ludwig who taught Kim to smile when she sang. "You have beautiful teeth and the audience should see them," she said. Besides learning to smile when she sang, Kim learned little by little to smile at her surroundings, and soon she would be smiling as brightly as she ever had. She didn't know exactly what the future held for her, but in July she would be going home—not to Indiana, but to Korea.

Early during Kim's time in Vienna, the U.S. ambassador to Austria had attended a party given for Fulbright students. When Kim was introduced to him, he asked how it was that she had an American grant, yet looked Korean. It was the wrong question to ask! When Kim finished her story and told the ambassador she still had a father and sister living in Korea whom she had not seen since she left the land of her birth, the ambassador asked Kim if she would like to see them again.

Her answer was predictable, and out of his own pocket Ambassador Humes provided the necessary air fare. This greatly encouraged Kim, and she began to plan her summer activity around this exciting new event. Yet there were still some unanswered questions, to which Kim didn't begin to find the answers until Christmas of 1973.

Paul Little, an Inter-Varsity speaker, was visiting and speaking at Schloss Mittersill. I made an appointment to see him on Christmas Day. I told him I didn't know what I was going to do after the Fulbright was up, and that I was wondering if I should ask for a renewal or try to finish my doctorate at I.U. I told him I didn't have to make a decision to renew until January 31. Then Paul said something which reminded me of how God had worked for me in the past. "The Red Sea has a way of opening up just when you get there." I had been reading in Genesis and Exodus with my Optacon and had seen how God provided. It was neat to learn again that God never supplies sooner than necessary.

During her Easter vacation, when Kim again visited Schloss Mittersill, Stacey Woods' wife added a further dimension to Paul Little's words. "Things look hard right now," she said, "and you don't know what the future holds for you. Remember our life is like a rug. God looks at the finished product from the top side. But we see only the loose ends from the underside."

It was also during Easter vacation that Stacey Woods told Kim he was writing Paul Little, one of the organizers of the Lausanne Congress, to get an invitation for her to come and sing. And sing she did! When a pastor from a Southern California Presbyterian church disembarked in Los Angeles after the congress and was asked by his Christian Ed director what impressed him the most, the pastor said, "I'll tell you the two things that impressed me most. One was, I can't remember what the one was. The other was a blind Korean singer named Kim Wickes. She is the most fantastic singer I have ever heard. I immediately booked her to sing in our church."

At the beginning of the congress, Cliff Barrows prayed with Kim and thanked the Lord for leading her through the time of testing she had in Vienna, then said, "Now, Lord, there are many uncharted paths ahead. Please pilot Kim."

Before, Kim had been committed to self—not vanity or a selfish pursuit of pleasure, but to a basic understanding of her own values. Besides the urge to know, she strove for a realistic understanding of her potential and her strengths. Yet she found this pursuit self-defeating.

I knew that my happiest and most calm times were when I prayed and let God help me with a decision, when I wasn't running my own life trying to figure out what would happen next, when I lived my life by faith and wasn't concerned about my own achievements. When I talked with Paul Little I told him I would dig ditches if that was what God wanted. I had learned that the really happy people are those who love and obey God.

Kim was as good as her word. She reached a decision to temporarily, perhaps indefinitely, shelve her doctorate program in favor of being a full-time religious vocalist.

Although Vienna was a necessary and important part of God's plan, it was Lausanne which became the springboard to Kim's career. When she left the congress, Kim had commitments to sing at Billy Graham's twenty-fifth anniversary celebration in the Hollywood Bowl, as well as at the 1974 Norfolk Crusade. In addition, she had invitations to sing in churches from Canada to Florida, and from California to Virginia. Yet before she was to begin this new venture, she had one important stop to make—Kimpo International Airport, Seoul, Korea.

It was fitting that the same newspaper which brought Kim and her father together through correspondence should now cover the reunion. Under the heading "Blind Vocalist Meets Real Dad After 21 Years," the August 9, 1974, edition of the *Korea Times* ran this article:

A dramatic event was staged at a cloth shop in Yongdong market yesterday morning when a 66–year–old farmer and his abandoned daughter from the United States were reunited for the first time since they parted 21 years ago. The 27–year–old daughter couldn't see her father's face because she is blind. . . . "Are you my real father?" asked Miss Wickes as they embraced. "Sure, I'm your real father. You remember our old home . . . and when I gave you two persimmons," replied the father in a choked voice.

"Yes, I remember," said Miss Wickes through the interpreter. "I have many memories of our family. Now it is my desire to make you believe in God."

Miss Wickes sang hymns last night for some 600 high school students who are participating in a training Youth for Christ program. [This was part of EXPLO '74, sponsored by Campus Crusade for Christ.] She will visit her father's village and today she will meet her sister, Mrs. Kim Eun-Suk, 34.

Kim's reunion with her father, and later with her sister, seemed to have a cathartic effect.

As we ate a special dinner, my father wanted to feed me with chopsticks. I sensed he wanted to express something, but couldn't. He just held my hand. I felt sorry for him.

When I met my sister, she said, "Sorry I couldn't have saved your eyes." I felt she had carried guilty feelings. I told her not to feel bad, that this was God's plan for me, and that His way is best.

I enjoyed my sister and meeting her three children. When we left she said, "Let's meet again."

For the next four weeks, Kim (when she wasn't singing in churches or taking part in EXPLO '74 activities!) played the part of a typical tourist. She wrote Eva about all the sightseeing she was doing. This included visiting Mr. Holt's grave, looking up friends from the Holt Agency, swimming, and shopping—and then it was over.

She said her last farewell to her father and sister, sang her last concert, climbed into the silver jet, and sat back. Her mind was filled with all that had happened since she left Korea the first time on that cold November day in 1957. Only this time there was no orange juice or crying babies. She had a little fear of the future, but not much. A friend had given her a promise from Jeremiah 29:11:

> For I know the thoughts that I think toward you, saith the LORD, thoughts of peace, and not of evil, to give you an expected end.

13. If I Could See . . .

After I concluded almost four weeks of interviews with Kim, I took her to lunch at a Mongolian restaurant. We couldn't get kimchi, so we got the next best substitute. As we ate and relaxed from the pressure of interview questions, I casually asked Kim what she would most like to see if she could. Her answers will be with me forever.

> I would like to stand outside on a clear day and look into the mountains. I would like to see the stars, a waterfall, and the display of colors in the spring. I would like to see a Southern California sunset, and blond hair.
>
> I would like to see how images are transmitted on TV, and I would like to see some of the TV specials, like the Apollo moon landing. I would like to see the human body, outside and in.
>
> I would like to read a score of music, to see the faces of my special friends. I would like to see a baby when it is first born, to see if it is really wrinkled and ugly. And I would like to see a fat Christmas tree at Christmastime.

Like few people I've met, Kim has learned well the art of intensification—of giving herself totally to her environment. Her darkness has indeed become light. This fact is never so evident as when she sings or plays the piano or organ. Because she has pushed hard to reach the high ideals and destiny which God has for all those who belong to Him, Martin Luther's dictum is delightfully true in Kim's life:

> When a man's natural musical ability is whetted and polished to the extent that it becomes an art, then do we note with much surprise the great and perfect wisdom of God in music, which is, after all, His product and His gift.

14. Adding Thirty-Two Years

*B*y way of introduction, let me say that I'll summarize the years between the original book until now by two criteria: chronology, more or less, and topic. As you can imagine, summarizing thirty-two years of globe-trotting, meeting people of all strata, and learning from unique circumstances is a monumental task! Yet, it must be time for it.

In September 2006, Dr. Noah Hutchings of Southwest Radio Ministries of Oklahoma City was given permission to reprint my book, *Kim*. Now it is May 2007, and he is ready to do the printing, at which point, his assistant wisely suggested that I write an update. I told Dr. Hutchings, "I wish we had thought of that while waiting on the printing, but *now, you* have to wait on me, as I'm holding up the show."

As I think of this, however, it occurs to me that such is how life on earth goes. For example, the children of Israel, living in Egypt, had heard all their lives that they'd some day go to the land that had been promised to their forefathers, a land, by the way, that they had never seen. Even though they had heard it for generations, they had to rush out when the night of departure finally arrived on that first Passover. Likewise, I too had to rush when told, on November 22, 1957, that I must leave the orphanage in Korea to go to America. Quickly, I left the public school, rode the bus to Seoul, and experienced my first plane ride, landing in the United States on November 28.

In this day of abundant e-mailing in place of hard copy writing, here I go, attempting yet another daunting task of writing! You realize that the old axiom among musicians is, "Singers resonate where their brains are supposed to be"!

During my graduate years at Indiana University School of Music, my voice teacher had said that I'd have to figure out some way of putting my "good mind" to use. How accurate he was! Ministry—often facing situations that no human predecessor, to my knowledge, had faced—forced me to extra prayer and stretching the mind to the max. I'll try now to share some of the cameos of what could be titled "Continuation of the Adventure."

As Grace Stimson, a longtime friend from my Wheaton Academy era, says, my physically weakest part is the sinuses, which are infected right now; thus, I pray for the Lord's strength and help to manifest greatly in my weakness.

Since the original book ended with chapter thirteen, I have continued here with chapter fourteen. Here we go!

15. Lessons Learned from Rejection

*I*n this effort of reporting the last thirty-two years since the book was first published in 1975, I believe the Lord would have me deal with the issue of rejection first. You recall that the Fulbright Commission had flown the finalists among the singers to New York, so that the judges could see us perform in person. After the audition, the committee asked, "How will you, being blind, manage in a foreign country?" That was a good question, and I think I answered something like "I'll pray." I didn't know how else to answer. That first time, I made it only to the finalists, not actually being awarded the scholarship.

During the next year at Indiana University, however, I learned the need to think of other factors; e.g., Dr. Winold's idea of applying next time to go to a country, which would necessitate a different language, would narrow down the competition. Because I was speaking German as if I had grown up in Germany, Dr. Winold's suggestion was a brilliant one. Of course, retrospectively, I know that the Lord was providentially timing the place and the year, so that I'd be positioned to sing at the International Congress on World Evangelization in Switzerland. This was being planned for July 1974, and I had no knowledge of it when applying for Vienna. If I'd been awarded the Fulbright the first time I applied, I'd have been too early and in a country which was farther from Switzerland. "Jesus doeth all things well."

In my crisscrossing this wonderful United States and the world, I've noticed that people sometimes have the idea that those of us who stand at the podium never experience rejection, assuming that it seems whatever I do turns out well.

To this type of thinking, I say, "No glory without first the grub." Since there is a certain amount of subjectivity in one's taste, what one judge may consider to be the best voice may not be the one rated best by every judge. Even in the matter of voice, one European once commented, "Yours isn't anything special." I share this because it seems that hardly anyone gets through life without hearing some kind of discouragement. By now, we all know about Fred Smith of Federal Express, Bill Gates of Microsoft, Albert Einstein, and Thomas Edison, just to name a few. Mind you, I'm not putting myself in their category; rather, making the point that even the most gifted folks hear some disparaging comments.

How should one handle such rejection and discouraging words? I choose to believe in the uniqueness of each person whom God creates. No two people in all of history are ever alike. No other human can be and do exactly what I'm sent to earth to be and do. I cannot please everyone at all times. No, my job is to please the Lord, who is my guide and helper and is responsible for me. Philippians 1:6 ever dwells in my heart: "Being confident of this very thing, that he which hath begun a good work in you will perform it until the day of Jesus Christ." In every situation, especially when facing rejection, I ask the Lord the question, "What are you trying to teach me now through this?" Sometimes, answers don't seem to come until years later. I guess that's why the old song says, "We'll understand it all by and by." Some questions, I'm convinced, won't be answered during this earthly life, but the Lord will answer all, when we get to Heaven.

Speaking of Heaven, I think my biological dad will probably be there. Many of you have asked about him. In his last letter to me, he had said that he prayed, a word which he had not mentioned in previous letters; therefore, I hope that meant he prayed for Jesus to enter his heart. When he threw me into that river in Korea during the war, I never considered that as rejection. I always understood how desperate life was with no food, no home, no hope of anything except by begging. Instead of rejection, I took it to be the only way of sparing indefinite suffering. Humanly speaking, there was no way out, but that's when God's plan can go into action. In my years of concertizing, I've met soldiers who were present after two little girls had been thrown in a river by their dad, and only the blind one was pulled out. Rejection? No, just a springboard for God's plan!

The dramatic story of this rescue, I've been told by so many, would be such good material for a movie. Indeed, WorldWide Pictures flew me out in January 1976, from Wheaton, Illinois, to do a screen test, and a script had already been written; however, it apparently wasn't God's will, or at least, not His time. Ruth Graham had said that the theme song for the film should be "O Love That Wilt Not Let Me Go," the hymn by blind George Matheson, which I sing frequently. There were some parts of the script which didn't seem quite accurate to me, so I said that if the movie were made, it should be done right. A few years later, a script for a fifty-seven–minute teleplay was written but that film was never made. In my opinion, God's will was done.

The funniest part about this subject, however, is the comment made during the screen test for my playing my own part; i.e., "You don't act blind enough!" The person wanted me to grope for the chair, before sitting down in it. However, I didn't grope for it. I just found it and sat in it without thinking. My reply was that there would be plenty of scenes to demonstrate my being blind; e.g., when someone walks me to the podium and hands me the microphone to perform, when someone walks me to the gate of an airplane, when a friend reads instructions or mail to me, etc. According to my realistic thinking, not every scene had to show that I'm physically blind.

Now in May 2007, I see the wisdom of Dr. Hutchings's reminder: "It ain't over until it's over." Even many non-Christians on airplanes with whom I've shared my life story have said, "Your story just has to be made into a movie!" God, who knows the end from the beginning about every subject and everybody, is the only one who knows the final outcome on this topic. I don't know how to make things happen; however, I know that the Lord does all things well, making everything beautiful in His time. I think that he who stated that I didn't act blind enough perhaps wouldn't have that assessment today. I find that I am more careful now than in the past about being sure to sit in the center of the chair instead of sitting on one side or the other. I believe, as we grow older, we learn to be more careful of dangers which we hadn't thought of when we were younger. Regarding many aspects of my life, I find that my *modus operandi* is, "Better safe than sorry."

Do I think the movie of my life would be glorifying to God and a blessing to people? Yes. Do I know how to get it done? No. As far as I'm concerned, "I serve you, Lord, the best I know how, here and now." What I mean is, all of us should function where He has put us. Movie or no movie, like any other issue, is up to the Lord. I'll accept His will. In my way of thinking, not making a movie isn't a rejection. After all, I am God's responsibility, so let Him do as He wants with me. He can turn what people would call rejection into something good. God alone can turn a disappointment into a blessing.

16. The Rose

As thy days, so shall thy strength be.

—Deuteronomy 33:25

While I was singing at the National Religious Broadcasters Convention in Washington, D.C., on a dreary January morning, the Lord showed a sign of His favor in the form of a rose. To the widow friend with whom I had shared a room in order to minimize expense, I said, "I'd give a lot to touch and smell a fresh flower right now." Just then, there was a knock at the door. It was Lyn, who had a rose in a vase in his hand. I asked, "Where did you get that?" His reply was, "Last night on my room service tray, there was this flower, and since I have to leave for the airport now, and you have to stay here, I thought you might enjoy having this rose." I said, "Lyn, I had just said how I'd give a lot to touch and smell a fresh flower!"

When I tell this story in concerts, I remind the audience that the God of the universe, who knew that I'd want a flower at that moment, had already prepared on the previous night to have my friend order room service, arranged that tiny vase with a rose to be on a man's tray, scheduled Lyn's flight to be early the next morning, and put it on his heart to take the flower to me, knowing the weather would be dreary and that I'd utter a desire for a fresh flower. It is possible that the room service worker assumed that Lyn was a lady's name. Perhaps, all this is a small matter to some; however, to me, the rose was a special sign of the Lord's granting even the smallest favor at the right time. The verse that I associate with this event is Deuteronomy 33:25: "As thy days, so shall thy strength be." I wasn't feeling all that strong for singing that morning, but that small flower's arrival gave me a boost. I knew that God was there, perfecting His plan.

However, don't assume that every wish in my life is always granted so quickly. Since some desires are not granted, that makes the story above so special. My rose experience was yet another example of God's faithfulness. Even though not yet manifested, I pray daily for the miracle of sight. I know that Jesus, who cleansed the leper so long ago, is the same healer today. Since He told the leper, "Be thou clean," I pray that He says to me, "Be thou seeing." Sometimes faith teachers say, "Act like you already have what you're believing for." My friends and I truly think that I'm doing that. According to my friends, I act more sighted than many sighted folks do.

On one occasion, I did a foolish thing in trying to act like I already had what I'm believing for. A Delta Airlines agent had put me in the Memphis Delta lounge, saying he'd return to board me on the flight. Instead of waiting for him in the seat, where he had put me, I started walking toward the back of the room, where I found a door. Without thinking of anything but trying to act like a sighted person, I turned the doorknob and stepped into another area. The door promptly closed behind me. It wasn't until then that I realized the stupidity of my behavior and prayed that the door hadn't locked. If it had locked behind me, there is no telling how the agent would have found me for boarding! There could have been staircases or any number of unknown dangers in that narrow hallway. Thank the Lord! The door had not locked behind me. W-h-h-e-w! That poor agent didn't have to experience a heart attack at not finding his blind passenger! I apologized to the Lord, asking Him to forgive my sin of presumptuousness.

I still believe in the Lord's miracles. Meanwhile, I don't sit and wait for my eyes to see. Remember, each of us must serve Him to the max with that which He has given. He will not hold us accountable for what we do NOT have with which to work, but He will hold us responsible for what we do with what we DO have.

17. Setting Up Office and Apartment

After living out of a suitcase for two whole years following the Lausanne Congress, it seemed that the Lord was leading me to a different mode of ministry. With the exception of a few homes in various parts of this country where I could periodically recuperate, mine had been a schedule of constant travel. Mr. Jim Barnes, who had served as a vice president of Youth for Christ International in Wheaton, Illinois, had done most of my scheduling. By 1976, he felt that his purpose in that capacity had been fulfilled.

Meanwhile, I was meeting many wonderful Christian businessmen, from whom I was learning so much, particularly as the bicentennial year, 1976, with all of its celebrations, was upon us. Time and space won't permit my telling the myriad of details about 1976. However, suffice it to say that Mr. Barnes then went to work for one of the businessmen whom I had met in the South.

Birthing any new idea is very major. While I've never given birth physically, this ministry with which the Lord has entrusted me has required great energy, care, and ingenuity. Kim's Ministries is my "spiritual baby."

Great things seem to have been accomplished during 1976, a year that had begun by fasting. I still need more discipline in the matter of fasting, even at this writing, and desire to do more of it than I manage. During the first three days of 1976, I partially fasted, seeking the Lord's direction, asking specifically that He'd close all wrong doors and open only the right one, so that I couldn't make a wrong choice.

Some of the wonderful business people whom I met during 1976 included Mr. D. G. Seago, of West Memphis, Arkansas, and Mary Crowley of Dallas, Texas. Having attended Lausanne Congress herself, Mary had heard my singing there in 1974 and had already invited me to sing at most of her Home Interiors and Gifts seminars around the country.

When I was singing at one Home Interiors seminar, Emma Lee Oltermann was being honored as the top manager. At lunch, I sat at her table and told her that I like "hanging around number one." I believe that we become like those with whom we associate. I want to be around WINNERS so that I might learn to be one also! (If we hang around skunks constantly, we'll act like skunks!)

Emma Lee's husband, James, had served as a Marine in the Korean War. After graduating from the U.S. Naval Academy at Annapolis in 1950, he was commissioned into the U.S. Marine Corps. Immediately following his officer's training at Quantico, Virginia, he was sent to Korea. I have the utmost respect for the military, especially for those who served in the Korean War. Emma Lee and James have been my friends since 1976, during which time I've sung at their daughter's wedding, visited for weeks in their home, and hosted them in my home many times. Also, they have driven long distances to attend my concerts all over Texas, and we are prayer partners, being free to phone each other at any hour of the night.

Before going on to tell about setting up my office, in which Mr. Seago had a crucial role, I'd like to insert what a Home Interiors manager friend, Blanche Boren of Memphis, Tennessee, wrote in her book about those hurried days of establishing my first home.

With her permission, following is that excerpt from her book, *Thorns to Velvet:*

"Was Blind But Now I See"

The eyes of your understanding being enlightened; that ye may know what is the hope of his calling, and what the riches of the glory of his inheritance in the saints.

—Ephesians 1:18

A few years ago I met a young, beautiful Korean girl who was blind. I was reminded of a poem I had heard about one who whined even though he had two eyes when others were blind.

Kim was blinded by a bomb during the Korean War. She was in an American orphanage and was adopted by an American family named Wickes. She went to college and majored in music. She travels all over the world sharing her beautiful voice in song, praising her God.

I had the pleasure of helping her set up her first home and office in West Memphis, Arkansas. What a joy it was for me to see how God worked in her life! Such courage and determination I had never seen!

It was pouring down rain. We went from one apartment to another. When the owners or managers learned she was blind, they didn't have anything available. On our last stop as we were leaving a man stopped us.

He asked, "Are you Kim Wickes?"

"Yes, I am," she answered.

""I met you at a church concert; what are you doing here?"

She said, "I am looking for an apartment."

He answered, "I own these townhouses."

We went back in and the lady told him they didn't have any available. We left and came to Memphis to buy furniture although she had no apartment to put it in.

Kim asked me to name three furniture stores. Of those I named, she chose one. As we were coming across the bridge toward Memphis, it was still pouring rain. Kim said, "Blanche, you drive, and I will pray for a Christian salesman and a sale."

I said, "Kim, you don't have a home to put this furniture in."

"We will. God will provide."

We drove up in front of the furniture store still in the rain. A young salesman came out with a large umbrella to help us in. He had been saved at one of her concerts a year earlier at Bellevue Baptist Church. We bought a house full of furniture, all on sale.

When we arrived home my husband said someone had called and asked us to call. It was the man at the townhouse. They found out after we left they would have a vacancy in three weeks. This was perfect as Kim was leaving the next day for a three-week tour.

Oh, how our God takes care of His children if we give him all the pieces and trust and never doubt His mighty power.

The person who had phoned Mr. Boren while we shopped for furniture was the manager of the apartments. She had said that there had been a bachelor who had put down a deposit on the last apartment. He was to return that afternoon to pay the rest of the first month's rent. I told her that I'd pray God would change that man's mind so that he'd prefer something else later. When he came to talk to the manager that afternoon, these were his exact words, "I think I'll wait on something later." The manager was so amazed! I knew the Lord was at work in the heart of every involved party. What fun to witness God's answering my prayers!

After Blanche had taken me furniture shopping, I had to go on a singing trip to Dallas. When I arrived in Dallas, however, Mary Crowley had been speaking with Cliff Barrows and was wondering if perhaps I should establish my home in Minneapolis, Minnesota, Billy Graham's headquarters. There would be more people available to help and to travel with me. I was uncertain. Mary said that nothing in life is really guaranteed, but she felt that the Graham team loved me and would put its arms around me. How wonderful that sounded to me!

While staying at the home of Gloria Armstrong, I fasted for a day. On that fasting day, the excerpts of scheduled Scriptures for the day included Psalm 147:16–17: "He giveth snow like wool: he scattereth the hoar frost like ashes. He casteth forth his ice like morsels: Who can stand before his cold?"

During the two years of living out of suitcases, and even earlier at Indiana University, the doctors had advised my moving to the South, where the winter furnace heat wouldn't be needed as long as it is needed in the North. The move was suggested because my sinuses were chronically infected. Upon reading this passage from Psalms about snow, frost, and ice, my answer to the question of "Who can stand before his cold?" was, "Not I!"

After making a visit to the Minneapolis office, I observed that everyone there already had work to do. Therefore, no matter where I settled, I'd have to figure out, with God's guidance, how others could help. In other words, all of us were treading on what Cliff Barrows had called "uncharted" waters. The Graham team was a wonderful group of friends. We all prayed for the Lord to guide me.

I had been praying for a south-central location within the continental United States, one which would facilitate air travel in all directions. As time passed, I learned that the area in and around Memphis is considered by many to be the heart of the Mid-South. Thus, in bringing me to settle in West Memphis, Arkansas, just across the Mississippi River from Memphis, God was answering prayer.

Setting Up Office

This topic itself could be a whole book. However, I'll mention the necessary links only. Mr. Seago was the president of Mid-Continent Company. His main office was in West Memphis, and I had asked him to serve on the board of directors of Kim's Ministries, Inc. For the first board meeting we met at Mary Crowley's house in Dallas on June 22, 1976. To me, that date is interesting because it was on June 22, 1960, that I became an American citizen. I was excited to see what God would do on this new leg of my journey.

I soon discovered that there would be many bumps on the road. Mr. Seago had hired an experienced Wall Street consultant, Rod, with his expertise in money management. He had instructed Rod to stay at Love Field to study some assessments about Mid-Continent. However, just as Mr. Seago was leaving to go to Mary's house, the electricity went out at the airport. Rod, not wanting to sit alone in a dark airport where he couldn't read, came along with Mr. Seago.

At the meeting, we all went around the table giving testimonies and rejoicing. I wanted to encourage the blind, the orphans, and the veterans, and we believed I was uniquely prepared for this type of ministry. When the question arose of what should be Kim's salary, I answered, "A hundred dollars a month." The men, probably trying not to sound shocked, said nothing. After a couple of seconds, Mary popped up and said, "Honey, you EAT that much." My reply was, "What else do I need money for?" You see, I had a lot to learn!

En route from Dallas to West Memphis after the meeting, it was Rod, the consultant, who brought up the fact that everyone was excited, but nothing concrete had been settled. "We don't even know where Kim will live," he said. His suggestion was that I serve as the company hostess for Mid-Continent during the week and then sing on weekends. In return for that, Mid-Continent would supply me office space and a secretary to do the concert scheduling. This idea sounded like a super creative one. Rod felt that my personality would be an asset to the Mid-Continent Company and, certainly, Mid-Continent would be great help business-wise to me.

As I write this in 2007, it now is obvious in hindsight that God pointed me in the right direction by giving Rod this idea. At that point, none of us could see all the involved details of implementing Rod's plan. Incidentally, Rod only worked at Mid-Continent for a year or two. It happened to be at exactly the right time for me. Just think! If he hadn't been Mr. Seago's consultant at that time, and if there hadn't been a power failure at Love Field as Mr. Seago was leaving for the meeting, Rod most likely wouldn't have attended our meeting! There's no telling how different my life would have been. Yes, all things did work together for good, even the airport's lights going out!

We tried out Rod's idea for three days. Before I flew to the San Diego Graham Crusade, the Lord indicated a clear red flag. I phoned Mr. Seago from San Diego and told him that the smoke in the office was hindering my singing. At that time, workers could still smoke at their desks. Mr. Seago didn't have complete peace about my serving as a hostess either. Fortunately, we both realized that some changes were necessary. Since smoke in the office was harming my voice, I couldn't sing my best for my Lord. When a small office suite became available in the building, Mr. Seago decided to donate it for Kim's Ministries to use. He said that I'd have to find and pay my own secretary. Thanking him for the office, I knew that I could trust the Lord for everything else. As it turned out, that space was free for about twenty months. After that I paid the office rent, relocating a few times but always in the same building. Within that time, I had a chance to "get my feet on the ground." During this period, Blanche helped me organize my first home, an apartment. I bought furniture without knowing where it would be put. Hiring a secretary in a town where I knew hardly anyone was very difficult. In fact, I knew nothing about hiring help. Remember, I'm a SINGER, and the old saying is, "Singers resonate where their brains are supposed to be!"

Oh! There was so much to learn! At the end of the first year of Kim's Ministries, I gave away every remaining cent. I thought that was what I was supposed to do.

Also, I never realized that not every person is organized. The Lord had surrounded me with wise friends at Wheaton Academy, Wheaton College, Indiana University, and in Vienna. I must have been a very sheltered girl. What a shock it was to me that a worker would inadvertently drop a bank statement in the hallway and not realize the mistake until some friend would see the paper on the floor. I had always just assumed that sighted people could see everything on a desk. That was a mistaken assumption. Now I can understand how sighted people can't possibly always see everything on a desk, even though they may be looking right at the object. Former employees have told me that one invaluable lesson learned from me is, "Never assume anything!"

At times I was disappointed in my workers. For example, an employee merely feigned typing. After I dictated letters to senators or pastors, my former secretary would tell me that all such letters went out on a certain day. However, when no response came, I phoned to see if the recipients had received the letters. I discovered that my secretary had only pretended to type and didn't even have letters to mail. As for employees, I choose to think on the good, dedicated ones and forget my bad experiences.

For almost eleven years, Mr. Seago's company provided wonderful phone service at Mid-Continent, where someone answered the switchboard. What a wonderful help that was! The Mid-Continent payroll department also figured out the proper withholding taxes for my secretary and me. This afforded me peace of mind in knowing that such matters were being handled properly. Again, what a blessing!

When Mid-Continent office arrangements had to change, I was able to help by sharing my office with Mr. Seago. He had helped me get started, so it was certainly a joy to help him when the opportunity came.

Years later, half jokingly, I'd say that my first gray hair appeared after the incorporation of Kim's Ministries. However, that is true. Of course, I'm not complaining. Nowadays, I also say that if I had known at the beginning of the ministry what I know now, I'd not have gotten as many gray hairs. One thing I've had to learn the hard way is that some people are organized and others are NOT! If I had not tried so hard to change the disorganized (pilers) into the organized (filers), I wouldn't be as gray-headed. Seriously, I have learned to accept the uniqueness of each person in God's world. We are not all alike.

Teachers comprise a group of people who are organized, and I praise God for teacher-type friends in my life. One such blessing is Marilyn Knapp from Wheaton, Illinois. Although she had heard my singing at Wheaton Bible Church Youth Choir during my high school days at the academy, we didn't meet until the summer of 1969 at Schloss Mittersill, Austria. You may recall that I went to Europe during the summer after my bachelor's graduation in 1969. Since we both liked music, were organized, and were desirous to serve the Lord, we became good friends. After our meeting in Austria, Marilyn returned to Wheaton to continue teaching at the grammar school.

In the summer of 1974, when I was again at Schloss Mittersill for a few days after my year in Vienna, Marilyn was working there again. I learned that she was going to Lausanne Congress, and she was thrilled to learn that I would be singing there. During the next two years, when I lived out of a suitcase, Marilyn's home in Wheaton was one of the oases for rest whenever my schedule would permit. It worked out well, too, because Youth for Christ's headquarters were also in Wheaton, and my scheduling was being handled by them.

As soon as Kim's Ministries incorporated, the Lord spoke to Marilyn's heart. In January of 1977 she left her teaching job at Wheaton

Christian Grammar School to come to help me. It was a real step of faith for her to give up a teaching job of many years to go to an uncharted path of sailing! For the first year, using her old Volkswagen, she drove us to many concerts, to the airport, and ran all the errands involved in setting up an office and living quarters. In return for that, the ministry just reimbursed her expenses but provided no personal compensation. After a year, with her funds being depleted and with the ministry becoming better established, I paid her a very modest salary. We were together 24-7, sharing one motel room when traveling, sharing one apartment when in town, and working together in the same office. With great dedication, she worked with me for nineteen months in this constant togetherness. Wonder of wonders, miracle of miracles, and praise to the Lord, we are still friends!

A Bible college in Memphis then was in need of her type of service, so she went there to work. All through these many years, however, we've remained lifetime friends. What a special blessing!

On some of those concert trips in the initial years, we'd use her car even though, because of some disorder, it put out heat in the summer. I'd always be in a long dress, adding to the discomfort of the hot mid-south summer!

It became necessary for the ministry to purchase a car, so I asked Mr. Seago's pilot to select a suitable one at a good price. I knew absolutely nothing about cars. He selected a Ford Fairmont station wagon which served well with lugging suitcases full of record albums, copies of my biography, and personal necessities. To purchase the car, the treasurer of Mid-Continent co-signed the bank loan with me, and the vehicle was in the name of Kim's Ministries, not in the name of a totally blind person. Explaining the whole ordeal of a blind person's borrowing from a bank to buy a car would have been too much, as all of us were walking on new paths. As soon as possible, I paid off that loan when it dawned on me that the years of carrying a car note meant more expense than the actual price of the car. I had named the car "To-It" because it was the means of our getting around "to it," whatever the "it"—the duty at hand—was. After fourteen years and sixty-two thousand miles, the car was sold when there was no longer a regular driver.

After Marilyn went to work at the nearby Bible college, I traveled for a school year with Mary Yoder, a special education teacher at a public school in Iowa. I met her at a Billy Graham associate evangelist's crusade where I was singing and she was volunteering. The Lord led her to take a sabbatical from teaching, and we prayed and traveled together. During that year, I learned a great deal while doing a weekly thirty-minute radio program that aired over ten large Christian stations from New Jersey to California. I taught Bible and sang on these programs. Listeners loved it, but the expense became prohibitive. Professional producers, who distributed programs for larger well-known ministries, wrote appeal letters encouraging listeners on my mailing list to support my ministry financially; however, recipients wrote me back saying that these letters didn't sound like Kim, and they weren't happy with such letters.

True, even the late Dr. Adrian Rogers of Bellevue Baptist Church in Memphis had said that I should do a radio program. He considered me a good communicator and the most articulate person he knew. However, I didn't see the need of doing something which would put me in debt. I had to ask the question: Does America need another program on her smorgasbord of spiritual broadcasts? Answer: not if it meant putting me into debt.

After a year of doing "Daybreak with Kim" on radio, I discontinued that, preferring to be the guest on others' programs. On one such guest appearance, Dr. D. James Kennedy of Coral Ridge Presbyterian Church of Fort Lauderdale, Florida, demonstrated very good thinking. To give me a two-minutes-left warning, he said he would gently touch my shoe with his. I told him that was very good—because he finished his sentence just as I was going to suggest that very idea. How refreshing to meet people who understand!

At this writing in mid 2007, I still believe that disseminating the gospel through the media is the most efficient means of reaching the largest number. Participating as a guest in others' established programs seems wise. Over the years, there have been several appearances on "The 700 Club," "The PTL Club" once, a few times on Trinity Broadcasting in its early period, along with numerous other programs, including radio broadcasts into North Korea and the Philippines. In recent months, God, in His faithfulness, seems to be bringing together Southwest Radio Ministries and Dr. Carl Baugh, founder and director of Creation Evidence Museum, in Glen Rose, Texas, into my life to accomplish furthering of the witnessing ministry.

For the most part of the traveling years, I've traveled without a companion, just alone. In doing so, I've had to depend on the Lord Himself to a special degree. After the tragedy of September 11, 2001, I'm particularly grateful for printed matter, radio, and television for spreading the good news of how the Lord works in the life of His own.

Keep in mind that there had to be a secretary at the office in West Memphis at the Mid-Continent Building where I was renting office space. She did all the scheduling of concerts, kept records to submit to the Mid-Continent accountant (who then prepared the monthly balance sheets), did correspondence, etc. When she had a question, what a blessing it was to be able to ask somebody in that Mid-Continent Company! I'd phone in almost daily and listen to the report which she would leave on a cassette dictaphone, and then I'd leave her any necessary response, dictation, suggestions, etc. The accountant of Mid-Continent set up the small accounting system for my ministry, and I use that designation system to this day, as I now do all such work myself on a regular computer. Before going on to that subject, I must share a bit regarding the move from an apartment to a house and how the Lord supplied the piano! All these demonstrate His never-too-early but never-too-late way of answering prayers!

18. *God Provides the Right Piano*

*E*ven during my time of living out of a suitcase with no home base, I began praying for the right piano. Mary Crowley had advised my asking for a used one and to check the newspapers. I then prayed for these specifics: a used, old Steinway Grand, at a bargain price. That furniture salesman friend, who had sold us everything at a discount, became a personal friend, so I told him and others to be looking for a piano.

During the week of Thanksgiving, a music store in Memphis phoned to say that they had gotten in a Steinway Baby Grand at a very good price, but that many people were interested in it, and that I really needed to put a down payment on it to hold it. En route to the airport to sing in North Carolina that weekend, I stopped at the store, played on the piano, and put down a hundred dollars so the store could put "Sold to Kim" sign on it.

Next, it was time to pray for the rest of the money to complete my purchase. By the evening of December 14, Mr. Seago had decided to help by paying the balance on it. As time went on, I learned the history of this piano. Made in 1922, it had been played by a lady of that generation who lived in Mississippi. Then it sat unused during the next generation. In its third generation, the teenaged grandchildren wanted to get rid of the piano in favor of more space in the living room for their rock music speakers. Thus, they had sold it to the store at a bargain price. The store said it was the first grand that they had ever handled. I left the old faded keys as they were. How thrilling to play the Steinway, its sound resonating throughout my apartment.

While I was away to sing during Christmas, however, a new office secretary, wanting to surprise me with a clean home when I returned, used furniture polish without realizing that it would streak the piano. We found it necessary to call the piano movers back to have it refinished. That was an expensive ordeal. We live and learn.

During the eighties, the keys began to show "arthritis," but I'd pray for them to keep working. Finally, in 2000, after almost eighty years from its original construction, my Steinway had to be rebuilt. I debated and prayed about downsizing to a smaller piano instead of having it rebuilt, due to the cost. However, Ted Smith of the Billy Graham team advised on the phone that it would be much wiser to go ahead and rebuild the old piano because of its value and beauty.

Remember what the specifics of my prayer for the piano had been? God answered every one of those adjectives: used, old, Steinway Grand, at a bargain price!

19. Moving from Apartment to House

After eighteen months of apartment living, I shared with my office secretary that I wanted to ask the Lord for a house where my vocal and piano practice, sometimes in very early hours of Sunday morning, wouldn't bother the neighbors. I was busy ministering out of town most of the time. When I returned from one such trip, the secretary told me that she had talked with Margaret James, a realtor friend, about my new prayer request. Margaret's daytime job was to work at Mid-Continent while doing real estate on the side. She'd often give me rides to and from the office building, since her own home was but a few blocks from my apartment.

Suddenly the house two doors north of Margaret's home went on sale by the owner. Margaret asked the seller if she could list the home. Connie, the seller, had suddenly become widowed when her husband died of a heart attack, and she wanted to move to Oklahoma where she had relatives. Margaret suggested I look at the house with her. I had often had supper at Margaret's and we both thought, "How handy it would be if we were neighbors!" I could walk to her home by myself with no trouble from Connie's house.

When Margaret and I walked into Connie's house, I could actually visualize living in it! Decision making is usually agonizing to me; however, of this house being right for me, I was sure. The Holy Spirit clearly helped me to picture living in it. No, I didn't hear an audible voice, but there was no doubt. Few things in life have been that clear to me. I noticed the arrangement of Connie's furniture as my mind placed my furniture from the apartment in comparable order as hers. Margaret joined in praying about the house. Having never bought a house before, I didn't know exactly where to start.

Since Mary Crowley's business was Home Interiors and Gifts, I phoned her, telling her about the house for sale. She said that I had wandered so much for so long that she thought settling into a house would be good. She said, "Every woman needs a home." She suggested that I talk with Mr. Seago, since he is "right there in the locale." He'd know best about the whole situation. She said he'd have to steer the rest of the board members, once he saw the house.

I began phoning Mr. Seago, but it was apparent that this was going to be a challenging hurdle. On my first call to present the idea of moving to a house, he said, "No." I was constantly praying and thinking. The next time I phoned him, he said, "I told you already that you can't afford a house." Knowing that he had my best interest at heart, I dared to ask him, "Well, do you want me to live in an in apartment all my life?"

I shared with him that the apartment rent was increasing regularly and that the house note would actually cost less than the monthly rent. The main financial issue would be coming up with the down payment. By now, he probably began rethinking the issue.

A few days later (the next time of my pestering him on the phone), I said that God had led me to some specific scriptures that morning in the scheduled reading. One was Nehemiah 4:14: "Fight for your brethren, your sons, and your daughters, and your houses." Of course, the context didn't exactly have to do with me, per se, but I was searching for the Lord's help, and found it in the phrase "Fight for . . . your houses."

In retrospect, I'm sure I'd not have had courage to keep calling

Mr. Seago had it not been for already clearly seeing myself living in the home. I was certain that assurance was from the Lord, so I kept driving the idea. I am a persistent person!

Another Bible verse of that morning had been Isaiah 54:2: "Enlarge the place of thy tent, and let them stretch forth the curtains of thine habitations. . . ."

When Mr. Seago heard that these two verses had been in the sovereignly-scheduled reading for that morning, I'm sure he really began seriously thinking. Mr. Seago really loves the Lord and the Bible. I didn't use this to trick him; the verses actually had been in my morning's reading.

Margaret kept asking me when I would be able to make an offer on the house. She was very helpful in explaining things about real estate, as I was as green as could be.

One day at about five thirty in the evening, I phoned Mr. Seago's office, and actually begged him to look at the house. He said, "Well, if I look at it, I want my wife to look at it with me."

I said, "I want her to look, too."

He said, "Okay, we'll meet you at that house in thirty minutes."

I was so excited! Next I thought, "Now, how do I find the key? How can I locate Margaret and Connie, or what do I do?" Again, I prayed, "Lord, please help me to find Margaret, and please let her have the key!"

Minutes were ticking by. Margaret had left the building after her daytime work and was "real-estating" who knew where? (This was before the days of cell phones.) A few weeks earlier, Margaret's sister had moved to West Memphis from Texas, so I phoned her. I talked so fast that she could hardly grasp what I was trying to say. I said, "Do you know how to find Margaret right now?"

She said, "No idea."

Then she said, "Wait. Here she comes, in my driveway!"

"Let me tell Margaret something. Hurry!" I explained to Margaret that the Seagoes were going to meet us at Connie's house in just a few minutes, so could she get the key, pick me up, and rush to show the house to them.

When we hurried to Connie's house, as soon as we walked in the front door, Mrs. Seago so naturally said, "Oh, Kim, your furniture would look so nice here." Since the apartment and this house had been built by the same developer, the color scheme was the same. While we went through the house, Mr. Seago was silent, but his eyes were taking it all in, I'm sure. He is one of these wise people, few in words, plentiful in wisdom, saying nothing unless necessary. As we finished looking at the house, he spoke two words, "How much?"

Connie replied that she wanted to sell it for forty-five thousand dollars, but that she'd let me buy it for forty-four thousand.

Looking back, I know the Lord had led Margaret to turn in at her sister's house suddenly, just at the right minute, to make this showing possible. Mrs. Seago's spontaneous response was positive. I believed the Lord would complete this project, directing Mr. Seago on how to execute the next steps.

I transferred every cent from Indiana University Credit Union, where a little was left after I had repaid all my student loans. This provided a start, but there was a long way to go. Mr. Seago made a conference call to all the board members and presented the idea of each lending me two thousand dollars, interest free, to be repaid as soon as I was able. We believed it was best if I didn't participate in the call so that all the people would speak their minds freely.

After the conference call, Mr. Seago told me that two advisors had some doubts. However, others were willing to double their loans, so eventually the house was bought. Marilyn and I moved in on Saturday, June 17, 1978. Since we were scheduled to go out of town the next day to give two concerts, we unpacked presto!

Of course, long before the move, I had planned where every piece of furniture would be placed. Nothing but the piano required professional movers. God had done another great thing!

In the subsequent years, I'd save from my modest salary, and each year I'd repay one person's loan. Everyone was repaid, except for two men who wanted their loans to be gifts.

Life changes. Workers move to other states, especially when their spouses are transferred. The Lord was apparently stirring the eagle's nest into discomfort. Without a regular secretary, transportation to and from the office had become a problem. For some months, I went by cab; however, that proved unworkable, because of having to pick up many others en route. Instead of being five or ten minutes to the office building, the trip could last an hour, and some of the passengers were smokers or heavy perfume users, and I'm very allergic to both.

As I look back, the world was rapidly becoming more technological; machines were replacing more and more human functions. One day in 1988, Mrs. Seago said, "Kim, you think like a computer. I think you could operate one. Why don't you find out about it?" Another friend, Phyllis, also thought that was a good idea and donated fifty dollars for it.

After I phoned literally hundreds of places about computers, specifying that I needed one a blind person could operate alone, the purchase decision was made. I keyed all my data into the computer and moved from Mid-Continent to my home. We had added a room to serve as the office for Kim's Ministries. It was April 12, 1990.

20. Going to Computer

Making hundreds of phone calls was necessary because I wanted to be sure of buying exactly the right computer and compatible accessories. The appropriate computer would enable me to work independently, not having to depend on a staff member. I spoke with both sighted and blind persons from throughout the entire United States. From each person I tried to pick up some bit of information on which I could build the next step. Truly, it was like constructing an edifice in my mind, while praying for direction before the actual purchase.

The IBM computer PS2 50Z is what I finally decided to buy. IBM had just produced a software program for reading text on the screen to the blind via a speech synthesizer which would be connected to the computer. Appropriately enough, the name of the software was Screen Reader, abbreviated to SRD. More often than not, blind people discouraged me from choosing this, saying that IBM should stand for "itty-bitty machine," and the software wasn't good for the blind because SRD required a small keyboard of its own in addition to the regular computer keyboard. Many blind people told me that they didn't like taking their hands off the regular keys to operate yet another keyboard. In my situation, however, I could visualize that small keyboard placed just as an extension to the regular computer keys, and couldn't see that being a problem.

Along the way of research, I met a young man in Memphis, Mark Shreve, who was eager to learn what might be available for the blind. He was quite helpful and excited when we'd share our discoveries and ideas. IBM's Division for the Disabled was enthused about the PS2 50Z and its custom-made Screen Reader software. To me, it seemed logical to buy both hardware and software from one company—an ideal technological "marriage." While waiting for the computer to arrive with Screen Reader and DOS loaded on it, I ordered audio tutorials from elsewhere for WordPerfect and listened to books on Lotus for accounting. While hearing these books, I made copious Braille notes that are still with me.

During this preparatory period, I asked Mom Wickes to come from Indiana so that she could read the thousands of names and addresses from my mailing list and Rolodex cards. She read during the whole last weekend of October 1988, while I was busy with concerts in the local area. All her reading was recorded on twelve hours of cassettes. At the computer's arrival, I typed in every word by listening to the tapes, but constant starting and stopping the player was necessary. Some sounds were indistinguishable and she was pronouncing names unfamiliar to her. Keying in the twelve hours of recordings took weeks! On some words I had to guess, and the list of names totaled more than ten thousand. In addition, months later and using different formats, I organized files for concerts and church visits, past and future.

Marilyn Knapp often said that it's a good thing that I like solving real-life puzzles. I'm not so sure that I really like doing that, but I am often forced to do so. Even though I hadn't asked for Mom's help in more than twenty-two years, she willingly fulfilled my request. Reading that many names would be a boring task, but I could think of no other way of putting all that into the computer.

Mark hooked up the computer on December 13, 1988, and how thrilled I was to hear its first three words, "in separation dot"! The

Braille manual, which I had studied, said that would be the first three words the screen reader should speak through the speech synthesizer and it did exactly that. I exclaimed, "That's a miracle!" For several days before Christmas, Mark would come after his daytime job and prepare the computer. He said I was the fastest learner of computer skills that he had ever met. I was so excited that it was truly fun for me then and continues to be as much fun even today.

Before Christmas, I offered Mark a check for his help, but he wrote "Not accepted by Mark Shreve" on it. Some years later, when he became a missionary to Papua, New Guinea, as a Bible translator, I became a regular supporter of his mission work. We've stayed in touch all these years. I sang at his wedding, we've visited together in Louisville and Dallas, and his family has stayed in my home. God's law of sowing and reaping is ever in motion. Mark didn't help me just to receive my help at a later time. While he was helping me with my computer, he didn't yet know of going to a foreign land as a missionary. Yet, God knew.

Before completing the computer setup, Mark had to move back to his home area of Louisville. What now? He put an announcement in his church bulletin in Memphis about my needing a computer helper. That particular bulletin ended up in the hands of someone who didn't even attend Mark's church—Dr. Richard Harruff. God was leading one step at a time. Richard had earned a Ph.D. degree and an M.D. degree, and was a forensic examiner at the Regional Medical Center. He had left a message on my office answering machine when I was out of town for months. When I finally returned his call, he cordially came to my office. Mr. Seago, who was sharing my office with me at the time, explained to Richard that I had a small business. My goal was to be independent, able to do all the office work on the computer myself. Mr. Seago and I could tell that Richard was most knowledgeable and efficient. With fear and trepidation, we asked him what he would charge. His reply was, "No charge." I thought, "More miracles!"

Mr. Seago said that I could give an office key to Richard so that he could come and work on my computer at his convenience. Since he had a daytime job, he often worked at night when nobody was there to disrupt his concentration. He embraced the challenge of computerizing my office as a serious project.

Richard, being a super thinker, could understand my goal. Consequently, I so enjoyed following his teaching, as well as discussing together the blueprint to accomplish that which was necessary to achieve our goals. Believe it or not, we had been at Indiana University simultaneously, but our paths didn't cross there. God knew when, how, and for what purpose He'd cause our paths to converge.

Before his moving away from the Memphis area in the spring of 1990, he helped me by moving the computer from the rented office space at the Mid-Continent building to my newly-added room at the house. He had pointed out that I should plan the move down to the tiniest detail, because nobody else could or would. Further, he offered that the computer should be moved extremely carefully. He, himself, would drive my Ford Fairmont very slowly from the office to my house. My job was to hold the computer on top of a pillow in my lap. How grateful I was for Richard!

After he introduced the idea of building macros in WordPerfect and Lotus, I built many in both. He programmed the database in WordPerfect Library and, into that, I keyed in the thousands of names and addresses. We designed several files in that database for various purposes, including questionnaires for scheduling concerts. To enable me to do the bookkeeping work, the monthly financial sheet had to be dictated while I'd transcribe the account numbers into Braille. I read each Brailled item with my finger and typed it into the IBM computer in order to print out that list for my tax accountant.

Even after Richard moved away, I built other Lotus macros for preparing printouts for the tax accountant and built batch files, usable up through year 2020 for copying Lotus files to floppy diskettes. Richard even created a customized program for the ministry's checks, each of which is in quadruplicate form. Although creating a "backup" of the hard drive had not yet been perfected, at least I was able to do all the correspondence and accounting. In addition, I was able to find any names and addresses by myself. God had been preparing me to be independent by the time Richard moved away.

Truly, this life is a walk of one step at a time, and the computer story is another illustration of that. How thrilled I was to be able to do the office work myself on the computer, which paid for itself in about a year! No longer did I have to pay for staff and office rent; expenses were now minimized.

By the end of 1997 a friend said that I needed to do e-mail, so I bought a clone computer with Windows 95. This computer's screen reading software is completely different from that of my IBM computer. The new computer uses its keyboard number pad instead of a separate screen reading keyboard for the blind. No other software used the extra keyboard as did the IBM, but I still like that one the best.

Finding trustworthy technical support for my computer has sometimes proven to be frustrating. Once a technician came and said that he could do what I needed done in six hours. However, he kept thinking of additional software and improvements that necessitated his continued coming. During this time, my computer performed less accurately. The technician's family often came along, and each one would read his own e-mail on my computer. They all enjoyed my free e-mail. Perhaps not all of the hours charged to me were for technical work. Finally, after having seen instances of less than good thinking, and after paying him $2,377.24, I asked him to restore everything on my computer as it was when he first came. He finally said that he wasn't able. I believe he didn't make notes of his actions as he went along, so nobody on earth knew what he had done. This was a major headache; however, in such valleys of life, I consciously tell myself to concentrate on good and generous helpers, as were Mark and Richard.

I've learned that the Lord blesses me even when others treat me badly. We are commanded to think on good things, as Philippians 4:8 tells us, "Whatsoever things are honest, . . . whatsoever things are pure, . . . whatsoever things are of good report; . . . think on these things."

As of August 2005, I e-mail on a Windows XP computer. I also occasionally listen to the live broadcast of Southwest Radio Ministries. My friend Sandra Perkins, Mr. Seago's former secretary, has helped me figure out some keystrokes. Sandra has a full-time job, so she makes an evening visit every six weeks after a long day at the office. I do some things by blind faith; thus, sometimes things work, while other times they don't. For example, the computer will speak the prompt, "Click here on the balloon to update." Upon hearing such a statement, I click by pressing "Enter"; however, I obviously didn't understand where "here" was. Not only did I not know where "here" was, but I also didn't know what my pressing the enter key did.

Thank the Lord for e-mail which enables me to stay in contact with missionaries in foreign lands, such as the Shreves! Another plus for e-mail is its ability to receive and pass along prayer requests from all over the globe. E-mail functions as a speedy prayer chain. Yes, when I have a prayer request, I send it to all my e-mail praying friends. Also, I pray for all equipment in my home, especially the computers, and for the angel of the Lord to encamp here to watch over all things and to keep them functioning. So far, I've received NO spam mail!

All the serious work—correspondence, financial records, addresses, and concert details—are still kept on the first computer bought in 1988. For ten years, many have told me to dump my IBM, but that is still the only dependable computer here for me. Thus, I pray it functions until the Rapture. I've met no blind "teachers" who know how to do accounting in the Windows environment, doing all that is required for tax preparation, as I do on the IBM DOS computer. I am not a computer "junkie," playing on one *ad infinitum*. Rather, to me, the computer is a means by which the Lord's necessary work can be executed, and for that I am grateful. In other words, my computer is a workhorse, not a toy!

Incidentally, I am writing this update on the IBM bought in 1988. How glad I am for not heeding the advice of the majority to bury it! May the Lord keep this first computer in perfect working order until He comes!

At this writing, this IBM acts as if it needs a new battery. It lost a whole week of time while I was gone for three days. "Lord, keep it healed and functioning!" I pray. Also, I have no backup system for any of the computers, other than backing up files from my old IBM to floppy diskettes. I keep praying, "My times are in thy hand" (Ps. 31:15). In numerous other passages, the Bible reminds us that He Himself is our keeper, as in Psalm 121:5. Therefore, I trust that He'll watch over the computers and keep them functioning until the Rapture!

21. Managing Hair, Make-Up, and Physical Fitness

As we eat up more years, the years seem to eat up some of our hair; thus, managing hair increasingly becomes a prayer topic. Over the last decade, gradually my hair has been cut shorter, but still is considered long, reaching below the shoulders. There really wasn't any problem until various coloring was applied, what I call "tampering," to hide the gray. Proverbs 16:31 says, "The hoary head is a crown of glory, if it be found in the way of righteousness." My thinking is that we ought always take care to be in the way of righteousness, thus not be worried about covering up the gray. However, most sighted people recommend coloring.

To color the hair, Sandra Perkins comes to my house every six weeks. At that time, she also adds new names to my e-mail list, downloads the new version of anti-virus software necessary biannually, and takes the annual corporation report to file. (I download its daily updates myself.) Since my birthday is in May and hers in November, we use the downloading time to take each other out for birthday dinner. Downloading the new version of anti-virus software takes a long time because my computer still uses dial-up. I do as much as possible personally, but filling out the annual report and coloring my hair require sight.

At concerts, I've often said that an angel from Heaven could come to fix my hair; however, God has given us minds and hands for executing such tasks. If my head is washed, it is by my own God-made hands. I then put in sixty to seventy rollers to curl my hair. Usually, this is a Saturday job in preparation for Sunday. After rolling my hair, I put laundry in to wash while I sit under the hair drier and read the Braille Bible. By doing all these things simultaneously, time is wisely used. I do my own hair care except for coloring, a trim every two months, and an annual perm. Friends say that the rest of me is so youthful, they don't want to see me with gray hair. For hair color advice, I listen to my sighted friends. However, I really prefer the soft and shiny texture of my natural hair. Coloring has caused it to feel stiff. As I've often heard, everything in life is a trade-off. Covering the gray may look better, but I think such chemical treatments are unhealthful.

Make-up is another area that illustrates the Lord's leading in every detail of my life. Getting my skin color analyzed was a real help along this line, but I didn't want to have it done. I thought only wealthy women enjoyed such luxuries. I was singing in Longwood, Florida, and staying with close friends. As usual, there had been concerts in the morning and evening, as well as some school chapel services on Monday. By Tuesday evening, my hostess really encouraged my going to Judi's for color analysis. I told her that if Judi could take us the very next morning, which was our only time available, we'd take that as a sign from the Lord. I thought surely Judi couldn't take us at such short notice; however, upon phoning her, we learned that the following morning was Judi's only empty slot of the week.

The next issue was that my hostess had never driven to the other side of town by herself; however, the Lord helped her to do that with no trouble. Judi had never analyzed a blind person's skin so it was a fascinating time for all of us. From her, I bought the correct color makeup and eight brushes. Since I was on the road, I didn't have the

Braille Dymo tape labeler; thus, I just had her to put one piece of Scotch tape on the first brush to use, two pieces on the second brush, etc., until there were eight pieces on the short last brush. Three shades of eye shadow were in identical containers. We then taped the eye shadow containers as we had done the brushes. Of course, I'd have to remember which to apply on which spot of the face and in what order. We likewise placed some tape dots on the outside of the color swatches in the book of recommended best colors for me, so that I could take that book with me when shopping for clothes.

Sometimes people remove my identifying markings, not realizing they serve an important purpose. This intended kindness reminds me of the necessity of communicating that there is a reason for each marking. Being orderly, task analyzing, and thinking things by association all aid in managing makeup, clothes, shoes, etc.

Once when I was singing in northern Tennessee at a rural church, a gentleman and his three children came forward at the invitation to accept Jesus as Saviour. After the service, he shared that he was a cosmetologist and hadn't been to church in years. After seeing my picture on the poster advertising the concert, he decided to attend. Wondering who did my hair and make-up, he came only out of curiosity. I wasn't aware of his presence in the audience, but because people frequently ask about makeup and hair, I spoke of having to use my own hands to do it all, fervently praying during the process. Since I have never seen makeup, I don't see its effect, but women say that it is worth doing. Since we are to obey our elders, I listen to this advice, but ONLY on Sundays and for concerts. The cosmetologist said that God truly is a great God, especially if He helps a totally blind person to do makeup by herself! As for me, applying makeup that time was surely worth it, since it affected his and his children's eternal destiny!

Some Europeans have told me that we in America put too much "stuff" on our faces. They say "stuff" results in a bad complexion.

Personally, I think one of the best methods for maintaining good skin is doing physical exercise to the point of sweating out the impurities. As in every subject, praying was necessary, asking the Lord to help me in coming up with an appropriate routine that I could do here at home. We all know that walking is excellent exercise, but doing that by myself outside isn't possible, so I had to think of other activities.

For many years, I'd work out three to four hours daily; however, that wore me out and took too much time away from other duties. Because of wearing out the machines, I'm on my third manual treadmill, second stair-climber, and second rebounder. Recently, I followed the suggestion of a personal trainer, who said to exercise no more than one hour daily. I go through my prayer list while on the repetitive aerobic machines. In that way, praying and physical training are accomplished simultaneously. On resistance training days, instead of praying, I count in Hebrew while lifting weights. I think exercising really is the best medicine.

In 1 Corinthians 9:27, we find Paul saying, "But I keep under my body, and bring it into subjection: lest that by any means, when I have preached to others, I myself should be a castaway." If I haven't exercised for days, I feel like a castaway. I find that serving the Lord with gladness is hard if I skip exercising!

While I'm on the subject of fitness, I'll mention that some say I'm a health nut. That's okay, but I'm not as faithful a health nut as some are. I just try to do the best possible with the situation in which I live. When we are sick, getting ourselves well again is typically our primary focus; consequently, ministering to others often becomes secondary. I believe we Christians must keep in good condition so that the work of the gospel can continue. To this I even apply 1 Corinthians 3:17: "If any man defile the temple of God, him shall God destroy; for the temple of God is holy, which temple ye are." Neglecting to exercise, eating things that God says not to eat, not eating what He says to eat,

and using poisonous, needless chemicals all contribute to much unnecessary illness. At least, such has been my experience. My sinuses
become infected frequently around Christmas when I am exposed to
candles and perfumes and eat more than a normal amount of sugar
and dairy products. Of course, I'm not saying that every ailment is
caused by external elements, but many health problems can be linked
to our choices.

On December 14, 2001, after being nominated as "a person of
inspiration," I was privileged to carry the Olympic torch en route to its
ultimate destination of Salt Lake City for the 2002 Winter Olympics.
Again, it was a good opportunity to witness, because the Lord answered
my three prayers. First, the Olympic Committee reserved the right
to have each torch bearer travel up to two hundred miles from home
to a torch-bearing site. This would mean travel and lodging expense
for me. I prayed that the Lord would let West Memphis be a place
where the torch would be carried. God answered my prayer. Second,
I prayed that the rain would stop. During the preceding weeks, we
had received so much rain that our town was at flood level. The rain
had to stop by the morning of December 14 . . . and it did! Third,
I prayed that the two blocks on which I'd carry the torch would be
a good smooth road, and it was. For two previous years, our town
had done repair work on Missouri Street, and my two blocks were
on that newly finished street. Of course, during that period of road
improvement, none of us had known about the Olympic torch relay,
because we weren't informed of West Memphis having been selected
until only two weeks prior to the actual event.

Although I'm obviously not an Olympic athlete, trying to be
physically fit provides a good platform for witnessing for Jesus. During one of my sinus infections, triggered as usual by sharing a ride
with someone using perfume, I was sent to a lung specialist by my
regular doctor. My doctor had done all he knew to do for me from

October to February. I knew in my heart that the problem wasn't in my lungs but was the sinus infection. However, at his orders, I went to the referred pulmonologist. He tested me and said, "You oxygenate like an Olympic athlete! No problem with your lungs." We deduced that while my two sinus surgeries had opened a path for drainage, the accumulation of draining mucus hadn't ceased. I thanked him for the compliment, but told him that as a singer I ought to breathe well. Besides, I should do no less, in order to sing of the Lord.

22. Constructing and Reconstructing

*Y*ou recall that the office was moved from the Mid-Continent building to the added room at my home in April 1990. Then, between 1992 and 1995, another addition was built with the hope of having someone live with me and help look after the place. Completing that annex was a huge trial, requiring three contractors.

Several months into the project, I discovered that the first builder was illiterate; he could neither read nor write. I, on the other hand, being blind and unable to draw pictures, was using my computer to put in writing every detail for the builder. What a classic case of "the blind leading the blind"! He left the place in an uninhabitable condition, saying that he was finished.

At one point I noticed the workers seemed puzzled, so I asked if they needed something. They said that they couldn't locate the studs because they had sheetrocked over everything. I replied that I could locate a stud by touch and sound. I had learned this two years earlier in Virginia while waiting for lunch at a friend's home. Men in the living room were banging on the wall to see where to hang a picture. Being curious, I asked them to let me see if I could help. Sure enough, the site of the stud felt more solid and the sound was a "thud" instead of a hollow noise. The men thanked me and said they could find the rest by measuring sixteen inches from that spot. That was an education for me, too.

This isn't to brag on myself, but to illustrate the truth found in

Proverbs 28:5, "Evil men understand not judgment: but they that seek the LORD understand all things." None of us has any ability, but that the Lord first gave it to us. Previously I questioned, "How can one understand ALL things?" When I was able to help my builders locate a stud, the verse lit up like a light bulb in my mind. Apparently, if we seek the Lord in all things, He gives us knowledge to match the situation at hand. This was another example of the providence of God, having prepared me two years earlier for locating studs.

When that new annex was sitting here in an uninhabitable condition, I busied myself with music and constantly stood on 2 Corinthians 2:14, "Now thanks be unto God, which always causeth us to triumph in Christ, and maketh manifest the savor of his knowledge by us in every place."

The second builder improved many things, but he, too, left without finishing.

The third builder completed the project. He was recommended by Brian Petty, a local heat and air man who turned out to be a faithful helper. For example, in October 2006, when a reliable roofer was needed due to a hail storm, he found one for me. Once again, I have to look for the good things in every trial, watching to see how God turns a negative event into a stepping stone for something positive in the future.

Just when the third builder had finished that second annex, the office space had to be reconstructed. The pipes in the attic froze and burst, ruining everything but the foundation and the rafters. I was beginning to wonder, "Is there no end to disruptions and frustrations?" This disaster happened on Saturday, February 3, 1996, when I heard what sounded like a jet plane taking off in my office. Fortunately, I wasn't out of town. What a mess it would have been if I hadn't been home!

I ran from the front end of the house to the office in the back, and realized that water was falling from every possible aperture from ceiling to floor. When I phoned 9-1-1, I was told to get a neighbor to help. I answered that both neighbors were in the hospital, and, it being a Saturday, my insurance agent was also out of pocket. I phoned my good friend, Ike Smith, in Collinsville, Illinois, and he said to call the utility company, a suggestion which I promptly executed. By the time the utility workers came on that icy day to turn off the water, it had run full blast for fifty-five minutes. I felt so helpless! Walking around my office, I knew there was at least three or four inches of standing water all over the large room. I phoned Pastor Kim of the Memphis Korean Church to say that I probably would miss church the next day due to what had happened. Since the men had cut the water off at the street, there was now no running water in the house. The only water was the small lake in the office.

After church the next day, Pastor and some helpers came to assess the damage. They told me the ceiling was sagging from the weight of the water. This meant finding a builder again to reconstruct the office. How grateful I was that the office furniture could be moved into the newly-finished second annex, even though it had required three sets of builders to complete! Thank the Lord for that annex floor's being one step higher, too! It is located south of the office. If the floor had been on the same level as that of the office, the water would have ruined the second annex as well. God had providentially provided the higher floor so that the office furniture could be moved into it during reconstruction of the office.

Time and space don't permit telling all the details of this crisis. Suffice it to say that the Lord is the Deliverer and Restorer. The carpet had to be taken away, cleaned, and put down again, not only in the office, but also in the adjacent bedroom to the west, into which the water had flowed. Painting had to be done all over. Insulation had to be blown into the attic and, this time, the pipes in the attic were to be wrapped to avoid another freezing and bursting catastrophe. Before putting on the finishing touches, the builder moved the furniture back into place. Therefore, when it was time to hang the decorative border, the workers couldn't reach above the furniture. While flinging the border over the furniture, they accidentally knocked a printer part on to the floor without realizing it. Being here at the office with them, I heard it fall. Reaching under the desk, I found it . . . in two pieces, which could neither be glued back together nor replaced.

Earlier, I had asked, "Wouldn't it be better to finish the work, including hanging the border, before putting the furniture back?" The builder replied, "Who is doing this job, you or me? I do this all the time. I know what I'm doing." In my eyes, however, he was not thinking in an orderly manner, as God does.

My biggest concern was moving the computer and restoring its original hookups. Those details are too hard to convey here, but perhaps you can imagine. Thankfully, months earlier, Sandra and I had found a huge pillow box to slip over the whole computer table, which Richard had built in 1989. The computer itself didn't get any water inside it, as there was no hole in the ceiling right above its desk. Praise the Lord! God, who knew this pipe bursting would happen, had prepared for protection in advance once again.

In working with builders, I've observed some things. One is that either people are in too big a hurry to do a job correctly or they have too much on their minds to concentrate on the job at hand. Once, during the first time of building the office, I found a hole, approximately four inches in diameter, in the newly-laid carpet. True, the hole would be under the desk, but I didn't want the concrete foundation exposed. The "blind" goes around touching things, and thus finds such errors. I thank the Lord that He led me to discover this hole, but pointing out such errors earns me the reputation of being a "picky old maid."

Another observation in building projects is the omnipresence of Murphy's Law: "If it can go wrong, it will."

From personal experience, I know that as soon as we do something without first praying about it, that's the very thing that goes wrong.

Currently, the second annex serves as a special place for missionaries, friends, and family. Thankfully, I continue to be healthy enough to take care of my home and guests.

23. Resurrecting the Flute

The first time of telling the story about the flute to a group of women, in April of 2006, I entitled the talk as "God's Neat Knits." God, who sees from above the tapestry of all lives, had worked ever since 1952, and in various places, so as to bring things together by January 2006. I'll try to be succinct.

At a Korean church in 2005 there was a ten-year-old boy who played the flute and who followed me around to help me get from room to room. One Sunday, I said to him, "Wouldn't it be fun if Miss Kim could find a flute, so that we could play duets?" By December 2005, I asked my dear friend, Jo Ann Vance, to help find a flute.

I first met Jo Ann on August 14, 2005, while teaching the book of Daniel to the ladies' Sunday school class at the First Baptist Church of West Memphis. Customarily, I have the members go around the room, each speaking her name as a way of providing audible identification. At the opposite end of the table from me, a voice said, "Jo Ann," and I wondered who that was. After the class, she introduced herself to me as the wife of the late Dr. John Vance, who for years had been the town's favorite chiropractor. To most people, she said she was known just as his wife, similar to my being known as "the girl who sings." I taught that class for two more Sundays, as well as a Tuesday class for three weeks, and Jo Ann attended both days each week.

Dr. Vance had died just two months earlier. Not until days after the funeral did I learn of his death, so I didn't attend the service or meet her. Now as I write this in May 2007, I've learned from her sister that Jo Ann perhaps would not have been at that Sunday school class in August if her husband hadn't died so recently. She was going just to Sunday school, not to the main sanctuary worship service, as she couldn't yet bear to go in that room alone without Dr. Vance because they had attended the services together for years.

As the weeks passed, I could tell that she was hungry for the Bible, as well as being a good organized thinker. She had recently retired from teaching school, and I could see that she could teach me much. For example, she said that there are two groups of people, filers and pilers, and that I definitely am a filer. In return, I couldn't help but share some biblical insights in our interactions, since out of the abundance of the heart, the mouth speaks. For several months, she did my grocery shopping and brought the items to my home, en route to visiting a dying lady nearby.

In January 2005, Jo Ann had moved away from West Memphis to Memphis. By December 2005, when I asked Jo Ann to help search for a flute, she told me that her sister in Virginia had one.

When Jo Ann inquired, her sister, Jeanie Sugg, said that Kim was welcome to it but that it would need refinishing as it had just sat on a shelf since 1954. During her school years, she had debated between learning the bassoon or the flute, and had chosen the flute.

On January 18, 2006, Jeanie sent the flute by UPS. Her e-mail gave the tracking number and said that the box was due to arrive by the following Tuesday, January 24. However, while I was listening to her e-mail, my doorbell rang. It was the UPS man, delivering the box already on Friday, January 20.

That evening when the flute arrived so quickly, I was so excited to try it out. With the exception of playing a couple of congregational hymns on a borrowed flute at Camp-of-the-Woods in 1966, I hadn't played the flute since participating in the Wheaton Academy band on the day of President Kennedy's death, November 22, 1963. Because of the expense, I never owned a flute; I always used school instruments. "Could I remember the fingerings?" I wondered. Miraculously, I could recall everything! Another miracle was that every note actually *sounded,* even though the flute was so old! It had a beautiful sound.

On January 24, Cliff Barrows of the Billy Graham team phoned me. When I shared that a flute had been given to me, he asked, "Can you play a melody on it?" I said, "I can play any melody you want." If the flute hadn't arrived earlier than projected, it wouldn't have been here in time for my conversation with "Uncle Cliff." He said that he was going to speak in Birmingham, Alabama, on January 31. As a surprise to him, some friends took me there on January 29.

The next day, January 30, Cliff took all of us to a *good* restaurant for a great lunch. As part of the surprise, I told him that I had brought the flute and it was in the car. Cliff said he had his harmonica with him, so we played duets in the parking lot even though it was a drizzly and windy day. We played appropriate hymns, such as "He Leadeth Me" and "Great Is Thy Faithfulness." I said that we had a small open-air revival meeting. The funny part was that it happened in front of a restaurant named "Tavern!"

After that fun trip, I played some solos in church, as well as some duets with the little Korean boy.

David Bingham, my piano tuner of thirty years, had recently told me of a band instrument technician in Jonesboro, Arkansas. So the next time my piano was tuned, I had David take the flute with him to Jonesboro.

This flute technician, James Halbrook, has one prosthetic leg. In 1972 his leg was amputated at the hip after getting caught between a rock and a heavy piece of machinery when James, then only nineteen, was on a job. After this injury, he went into band instrument repair in the summer of 1974, and has done well ever since. That was exactly the same time that I began a full-time singing ministry, following my Fulbright year in Vienna in May 1974. James's wife, a former band teacher, is also musical. While he has one prosthetic leg, I have two prosthetic eyes, so we both face the discomfort caused by man-made body parts sometimes fitting imperfectly.

David, my piano tuner, had always been pleased with James's work. While serving as a band teacher, David had taken instruments to him for repairs. Having known of James's good work for thirty years, he gladly made the referral. In addition to his refurbishing my flute from Jeanie, James has sold and repaired many more flutes for me. Having become a flute teacher, I am blessed to have a continual working relationship with a dependable technician.

By the summer of 2006 I returned to Memphis Korean Church where Pastor Kim serves. (The little boy had been at a different church, but my desire had been to encourage him to continue serving the Lord by flute playing.) In September, Memphis Korean Church asked me to start teaching flute as a means of outreach. I said I'd try. The Koreans are very title conscious, so they call me Music Missionary, although I prefer being called just Kim.

As I'm writing now in May 2007, there is a lady who is learning well, so we play duets once a month. Sometimes I arrange medleys for myself, alternating between voice and flute.

Since several in the church are interested in the flute, we have formed a flute trio and only the Lord knows how many more will join in playing together eventually. While writing this update, I've made an arrangement of "Count Your Blessings" for our trio to play. Our "debut" was on Mother's Day. Counting our blessings is always an illuminative exercise. Another neat fact is that all three of us have the same brand of flute. This means that the omniscient God had been working out all details to bring about this uniformity.

Jeanie had secured her flute in 1952 and then sent it to me in 2006. A second flute in our trio was bought in Korea in 1993. The third was purchased in Memphis in 2006. However, none of us knew what brand of flute the others had. Playing together as a trio certainly hadn't occurred to us at the time of obtaining the flutes. The fact is, if I had refused to teach the flute when asked in September 2006, none of these interesting facts would have surfaced. Would you believe that each one of us has a common syllable in our names? The shared syllable is "Eun," which means "Grace." Therefore, we call our trio "The Grace Flute Trio." The omniscient heavenly Father, knowing the beginning and end of all matters in the whole universe, sovereignly led all three of us to have the same kind of flute, unbeknownst to any of us in advance.

In summary about the flute, I marvel at how the Lord was working in various parts of the world and in different lives, in order to tie together the neat knitting pattern. In 1952, if Jeanie had chosen the bassoon instead of the flute, this tapestry wouldn't have come together. At that same time, I was in war-torn Korea as a begging refugee, scraping to eat anything that could be found—worms, crickets, grasshoppers, etc. Everything, even unpalatables, tastes the same when it is burned in a small fire of sticks.

When I was thirteen and an eighth grader at the school for the blind in Indiana, the Lord put in my heart the desire to play the flute. Moreover, God brought the piano tuner, David, into my life thirty years prior to Jeanie's giving me the flute. God also led me to James, the band instrument technician in the same town as David. James was led to his line of work the same summer as when the Lord began my full-time music ministry. Retrospectively, we can see God's timing in every detail. He began to show us His knitting the strands together by the year 2005, when Jo Ann came to the Sunday school class. How fun to watch the hand of God in all such everyday details!

Praise the Lord.

My teaching flute is another way to minister in the body of Christ. Although there is no charge for lessons, it is wonderful how the Lord balances blessings to return to me, as I try to give that which I can. Of course, that's no surprise because it is part of God's revealed design. "Give, and it shall be given." The lady with whom I duet monthly is kind to provide some fruit, soy milk, or whatever I need. Her family often transports me to or from church. I wrote Jeanie an e-mail, stating that her flute is now a "holy, set apart" one, since it goes to church every Sunday. Following our morning worship service for which I usually sing, we have lunch and then I teach flute.

Just as flute teaching illustrates part of God's design, sharing with each other as believers, the next chapter illustrates how various members in the body of Christ help each other.

24. Interrelationship Among Members of Christ's Body

I'm learning two basic principles about how the body of Jesus functions. First, we cannot give what we do not already have. Second, as we give, things are set in circular motion, so that not only the receiver is blessed, but also the giver is rewarded.

I often stress that each person must inventory his strengths and function to the optimum in a suitable capacity. To me it is a wonder that the Lord never runs out of patterns. Throughout history, there are no two humans exactly alike, as each person is unique. Scientists say that there are no two identical snowflakes either. I can't fathom the infinite creativity of God.

In a concert, I had said that I'd like to be an airplane pilot, but I knew that's not what God had equipped me to do. I also said that I was disqualified to be a cab driver. Afterward, my volunteer helper said, "Kim, you could be a pilot." I asked, "How?" She said, "You don't have to see. You just fly by instruments." I said, "How do you think I could read the instruments?" In realizing what she had said, she whispered, "Don't tell I said that." For twenty years I didn't tell.

The point is the Lord equips each person for a particular and individual niche in His church. I can't do what someone else is to do, and nobody else can fill the spot which God has cut out for me to fill. In order for the body of Jesus to function, each person must operate in his assigned niche. I can't be the driver of a car, but I'm responsible to do what I can.

My second observation is that the giver and the receiver are both blessed. On the occasion of teaching this principle at Memphis Korean Church, I illustrated by saying that the Dead Sea has no life, as it only receives without giving. On the other hand, the Sea of Galilee and the Jordan River teem with life because the water is in motion, giving life as it flows southward. Knowing that to be true, I must give in the area of music and Bible teaching, because these afford channels of service. As I do that, the Lord causes others in the church to bless me back.

For example, while I'm concentrating on writing this update, some Korean friends have brought food and earrings. What signs of Christian love! The food saved me time and energy so that I could concentrate on writing. Selecting earrings for me was thoughtful because that is one piece of jewelry that I use.

Regarding the issue of cooking, I've prayed for wisdom to manage food as simply as possible. Proverbs 30:7–9 has been a long-time prayer of mine. "Two things have I required of thee; deny me then not before I die: remove far from me vanity and lies; give me neither poverty nor riches; feed me with food convenient for me: lest I be full, and deny thee, and say, Who is the LORD? or lest I be poor, and steal, and take the name of my God in vain."

Using foods that are convenient and easy to prepare frees up time and energy for more important activities. I use much fresh salad, raw fruit, and some protein powder for shakes. I boil eggs and cook oatmeal on the stove. Sometimes I even use a juicer. I always keep frozen dinners on hand. After meeting me at my concert at their church in 1977, the Baker Group of Shaklee Company continues to donate their products for my use. What a blessing! As in everything in life, seeking God's direction for prudence is necessary.

During one season from Thanksgiving to Christmas, I gave away sixty-two cakes, which I had baked in a Crock-Pot. To do this, I had to crack lots of pecans. All that dusty pecan cracking led to a sinus infection and that meant friends had to bring warm soup to restore my health. Thus, we all give of what we can, and the Lord keeps the circular motion going.

Another illustration of how the Lord leads us to bless each other is shown by His sending Don and Joy Sample into my life. We met when I gave a concert at their church here in West Memphis. In the concert, I had stated that my biggest problem is transportation. Joy said, "When you need something, just call." Sometimes people say such words, but idly; however, in her case I discerned that she was a mature and responsible one who would keep her word. Being a literalist, I took her at her word.

Always I do as much as possible myself; however, some things in life just require God-made eyes. For the next few years, Don and Joy were kept busy as they assembled any new exercise equipment. I jokingly told others, "Maintaining my exercise equipment is their full-time job." Joy comes to give my weekly allergy shot and sorts my mail and reads to me only what is important, discarding all nonessentials. Even prior to her coming, I pitch received mail if I'm absolutely sure of its being junk. After all, Hebrews 12:1 admonishes, ". . . let us lay aside every weight, and the sin which doth so easily beset us, and let us run with patience the race that is set before us."

As Joy reads the payable bills, I put Braille dots on each one so that I know its actual information. That way, nobody needs to read it to me again. On that paper, I punch out from whom the bill is and the date and amount due. When I later write the checks, I put Braille notations on the checks, too, including check number, the recipient, due day, and the date and amount paid. Then, before filing each of the three copies of the check into the proper folders, I enter all this information into the accounting sheet on my original 1988 computer. From this and other worksheets, I print out a detailed description of all transactions for the accountant. Executing such work illustrates that the Lord grants us wisdom, when we ask for it, by literally believing His word, found in Jeremiah 33:3: "Call unto me, and I will answer thee, and show thee great and mighty things, which thou knowest not."

Historically, the LORD in this chapter is prophesying His wonderful plan of restoration of Israel in the millennium. Yet, devotionally, we Christians in this age can draw spiritual application. In fact, this is one of the framed verses, which hangs on my office wall. There are times in life when all I know to do is to point to the verse on the wall and remind the Lord of this promise. Occasionally, I don't even know what questions to ask, much less do I know the answers.

I keep only a minimal amount of papers, perhaps discarding too much. If a letter is to be kept, I notate on it in Braille; e.g., on a letter from Elisabeth Elliott, I put the date of her writing, her name, and a short summary of the letter's content. By so doing, I can do my own filing and future locating. Every file folder and label made requires my notating in Braille for me, as well as notating in print for the sighted. Thus, most steps must be duplicated. No wonder I keep only the necessary papers!

Joy's eyes are needed in selecting appropriate greeting cards for birthdays, get-well, sympathy, wounded soldiers, and various congratulatory occasions. I regularly keep a supply of cards on hand, to be on ready mode to minister by sharing them. Recently, when UPS delivered my order of a large box of cards, I opened and unpacked its contents, which were several smaller boxes of all the same size. After stacking them into four neat piles, I waited for the day when Joy would come to give me my weekly allergy shot.

When she arrived, she grouped on top of the desk the boxes by topics; e.g., one stack would be all boxes of only birthday cards. In every box of twelve, all the cards would be for the same occasion. For example, one box may hold a collection of "encouragement" ones, while another box would have only birthday cards. On file folder labels, I write in Braille the words "birthday cards, obtained on so-and-so day", or "sympathy cards, arrived on so-and-so day." Then, such Brailled labels are stuck unto the bottom of the matching boxes. I store the individual stacks of like boxes in different file cabinets, which reduces the number of labels that have to be read. One cabinet holds the birthday boxes and a different file cabinet holds the encouragement type.

People often ask me why I put labels on the bottom of the boxes instead of the top. To them feeling the Braille label on top of the box would be easier than lifting the box to feel the label on the bottom. My reason for placing the Braille markings on the bottom of containers is that lids might get mixed up. Since the bottom of a container is the holder of the cards (or whatever its content is), I'll always know which cards are in the box if the label is on the bottom. I also use this method in labeling cosmetics and food containers. By labeling and filing as described, a greater degree of independence is achieved. After all, everyone is busy with his own life; I resort to others' help only when necessary.

Just this month, I sent a birthday card to an octogenarian prayer partner, who was my office secretary at one time. Her birthday would come before I'd see Joy for the next shot, and I also had to pack for going out of town. It was fun to be able to find the correct card, sign it with nobody here to show me where to sign it, place in it the cash gift, type her address on the intended envelope, place the stamp and my return address label, and send it, trusting that the typewriter ribbon still hadn't run out of ink.

When I phoned the recipient on Saturday night, as is my custom, she excitedly told me that the card had reached her safely. She said it was perfect, and nobody would know that a blind person had signed it all by herself. When sending this card was necessary and nobody was here to help, I had prayed for the Lord to show me some way to figure out the right place on the card to sign. Would you believe that one half of the folded card was just a tad narrower than the other side was! Then I had to figure out which of these two halves was the front and which was the back. The card didn't have any raised design for my hands to distinguish front from back. After taking the right guess on that card to Jean, my prayer partner, now I know where to sign on that group of cards. Jean did say that her address on the envelope could have been a bit more to the left, as the last character, which is her apartment number, had been almost at the right edge. I appreciated her cluing me in on that and told her that made sense. I had begun typing as far to the right as I do on normal business envelopes, but her card was not as wide as they are. Those of you who have attended my concerts have heard me say that it requires extra prayer, more thinking, greater determination, and extra communication to serve the Lord if one must do so without possessing all five senses.

When writing a regular check by hand, I need someone with eyes to fill in the check before I sign it. My handwriting is too large for the small spaces on checks. Joy's eyes are usually the ones to help. Also, I'm blessed to have friends who are willing to provide transportation for necessary appointments and important errands. For instance, Joy has driven many times to Memphis for my biannual cleaning of my two prosthetic eyes.

A regular question is, "How does Kim eat so much but stay so tiny?" I say that I'm being biblical in eating heartily, because Ecclesiastes 9:10 commands, "Whatsoever thy hand findeth to do, do it with thy might." At least, that excuse sounds good. A frequent joke around here is that Kim will work for food; i.e., she'll sing; she'll play the flute, the piano, or the organ; or she'll teach Bible. Edibles are the very best form of wages for me!

In order to do what I can to help others, I participate in the Rosewood choir on special occasions, provide any programs when asked, teach Bible when requested, and play the organ or piano or sing for funerals. At the beginning of my ministry, it was necessary to be ready at the drop of a hat to sing at weddings. Now, thirty-three years later, I must be ready to do funerals at the drop of a hat. Joy teasingly says that funerals are our only social activity. I have also knitted lovely baby blankets for friends when they become great-grandparents.

As we give in the manner and in the area of our abilities, the Lord causes others to do the same. Thus, the body of Christ functions, demonstrating His creativity. What an ingenious and marvelously fitting design!

25. Trips to Israel

Christmas of 1980 was the first of my fourteen trips to Israel. That initial trip interested me because its primary reason was to hold a three-day revival at First Bible Baptist Church of Bethlehem. Some of my favorite Bible teachers have never gone to the Holy Land; however, they can see pictures and maps. In my case, actually traveling there proved to be enlightening. Seeing people accepting Jesus during the Christmas revivals in Bethlehem was particularly meaningful.

I'll mention just a few of the most special places I visited and share some poignant experiences while on the trips. First, not only did the trip to Megiddo open my understanding about the Old Testament battles, it also provided numerous opportunities to testify both to Americans in my tour group and to native workers. The Lord seems to have uniquely equipped me for relating with people in international settings; at least, many locals said, "You are one of us."

Second, singing *a cappella* "It was alone the Saviour prayed in dark Gethsemane" while touching the rock actually in Gethsemane, was such a moving experience. The text to the first stanza is, "It was alone the Saviour prayed in dark Gethsemane. Alone He drained the bitter cup, and suffered there (which I changed to "here") for me." It seemed that the Holy Spirit touched the heart of everyone in the group, because we kept hugging, praying, and weeping as we sensed afresh the agony of Jesus. Another awesome aspect about Gethsemane is the ancient olive trees. Since some of those roots are two thousand years old, they would have been the very ones that were growing at the time of Jesus. Wow!

Third, the caretaker of the Garden Tomb, seeing that I was singing for the groups and was blind, voluntarily unlocked the gate into the innermost part of the tomb and invited me to come in with him. (Normally, tourists look in through the bars only, perhaps as John and Peter did on that first Easter morning.) All of a sudden, many in my group followed me in, telling the garden guide that they were all my best friends! He showed me the hewn out place in the rock where Jesus's body could well have been laid. I lay down in that very spot.

Fourth, singing during worship services on the boat ride across the Sea of Galilee is so exciting, knowing that it is the very same lake on which Jesus walked and stilled the storm. Even today, storms can come up so suddenly, just as they did for the disciples.

Fifth, seeing the house of the high priest Caiaphas really helped in visualizing where Jesus was scorned and where Peter warmed himself . . . and three times denied even knowing Jesus. Interestingly, I heard in the distance the crowing of a cock on several visits there.

Sixth, I should mention the thrill of singing of Jesus's birth on Christmas Eve. My solo, "Gesú Bambino," was broadcast from Bethlehem Manger Square, right outside the Church of the Nativity. Having my neighbors here at home tell me of seeing that broadcast on the evening news was exciting! Although I had known of Israel TV showing part of that program, I didn't know that friends in America had been able to see it, too, on national news.

On some occasions, I spent a few extra weeks, after the normal tour period, and learned a little Arabic and Hebrew. During these extended stays, I'd sing for various other groups, even though I wasn't a member of them. One Palm Sunday, in order to give the gift of song to the Bethlehem Bible Baptist Church, I took a cab from Jerusalem

to Bethlehem. That afternoon, some from that church and I joined
the multitude in walking the path from the Mount of Olives, possibly retracing the very way Jesus traveled as He rode the donkey into
Jerusalem for His triumphal entry on that first Palm Sunday.

The trips to Israel developed into another channel of ministry.
I'd sing appropriate songs at the biblical sites, so that many in various groups said, "I'm not coming back unless Kim comes, too." The
Bible is an Eastern book, so some of the Holy Land's customs, such
as women carrying water pots on their heads, are reminiscent of old
Korea. Some enduring friendships were also made as we fellowshipped
together for several days on such tours. There were opportunities to
pass out tracts in Egypt on some trips. During my extended stays, I
also visited a school for the blind and gave some financial help and
winter clothing for wounded children in a hospital. Nazareth Baptist
Church is another group of believers for whom I've sung and still
help over these many years.

It would be impractical to write about everything regarding the
fourteen trips to Israel. I'll mention just two separate experiences.
The first deals with meeting a blind couple, and the second is how
the Lord got me to Allenby Bridge just in the nick of time.

Before my first trip to Israel, I received a letter in Braille from a
blind couple in Nazareth. Would you believe their names were Joseph
and Mary? On the radio program "Unshackled," they had heard the
dramatization of my life story. That program was produced by Pacific
Garden Mission of Chicago, Illinois. Upon receiving their letter, I
laughed at the names of the couple and at the fact that they were from
Nazareth! On that first trip at Christmas, 1980, I told the local guide
about having received the Braille letter from Joseph. The guide knew
of him; however, there wasn't an opportunity to meet during that
crowded trip with sightseeing and revival meetings combined. Later,
however, when I'd stay some weeks extra, I spent meal times with

Mary and Joseph, and Mary even sang in a ladies group for one of the Christmas programs at the Bible Baptist Church of Bethlehem. I'm grateful for those opportunities of fellowship because Mary went on to Heaven not many years hence.

The second story to relate is more complicated. However, it illustrates the faithfulness of God in spite of human errors. My story shows again that He delivers us out of our jams just in the nick of time. Remember, He is never too late, but never too early either!

Because the surrounding Arabic nations do not recognize Israel as a country, it is important that Israel not stamp a tourist's actual passport. With an Israeli stamp in it, a passport can never be used within Arabic nations. The normal procedure is for Israel to stamp a loose single sheet of paper, which is given to the tourist, instead of stamping in the actual passport itself. Once, when I was departing from Israel to return to America, I noticed that the separate piece of paper was not in my passport, a clue that the actual passport had been stamped. This was at the end of one of those extended stays, so I was flying back without being part of a group.

Another trip to Israel had been scheduled with a new group one month later; therefore, I had to figure out what to do about my passport. The next group was going to land first in Ammon, Jordan, and then cross the Allenby Bridge, over the River Jordan, from the Arabic land on the east to Israel on the west. I repeatedly told my office secretary that I thought there was an Israeli stamp in my passport; however, I couldn't see to show it to anyone. She said that she had shown my passport even to the attorney in the building, and he had assured her that there was no stamp from Israel, so Kim didn't need to worry. In retrospect, I ought to have questioned that the lawyer would have known what a Hebrew stamp looks like. Perhaps we humans assume that attorneys know everything.

With uncertainty about the lawyer's assurance, I went on to Jordan.

You guessed it. Of course, there was a big Israeli stamp, filling one whole page of my passport. When we landed in Ammon, the customs officer caught it. For the other twelve members of this tour group, this trip was their first. I, supposedly seasoned traveler to Israel, was now presenting a major problem. I wasn't permitted to exit from Jordan without a brand new passport, and the Ammon customs officials had kept my passport during the night. After clearing customs at the airport and riding to the hotel, the tour schedule allowed time for only a quick supper. Tourists have to get to bed early in order to be ready for an early crossing of the Allenby Bridge.

Since my new friends in this tour group were all concerned, we prayed together before bed, thanking the Lord for safe flight and asking the Lord to intervene in the problem of the passport. The tour schedule was such that I had to catch up with the group on the Allenby Bridge; otherwise, I'd miss all the touring days in Israel. If I didn't reconnect with my group, we had no idea how I'd even return to America, as all arrangements would necessitate alteration. The tour leader, Roger Jones, shared my dilemma with the group, stating that it could well mean I'd have to stay in Ammon some nights, separated from the group. Thus, he felt led to take up an offering to help defray that possible expense. The dear ones in the small group gave so generously that the offering was two hundred dollars!

All that night I kept praying, reminding the Lord that He had literally parted the waters of the Jordan River for the children of Israel long ago, and now I was asking Him to arrange my crossing the bridge over the Jordan River to be with the whole group on the very next morning, instead of having to cross it by myself days later.

Sometimes, we forget that the feast of Passover falls on a different day of the week than on the regular sabbath day. God's ordinance was that it be on the fourteenth day of the first month, and that usually falls around our Easter season. In this particular year, Passover was going to fall on Thursday. Our tour group had landed in Ammon on Tuesday evening. By the next morning, Wednesday, the group left to go to the bridge at four o'clock in order to be toward the head of the line of numerous busloads of tourists. I am sure that the group felt as badly as I did when they had to leave me, sitting all alone in the hotel lobby in the dark at such an early morning hour. We didn't know what to expect. How would we connect up again? Where? How could we communicate? (Please remember this happened before the days of cell phones.)

The local guide in Ammon told us that someone from the tour office would come by at eight o'clock to help me in getting a new picture taken, then take it to the American Embassy to apply for a new passport, and wait in line. The guide and my group left for the bridge. As I sat waiting alone in the hotel lobby, I heard groups speaking other languages—French, Italian, etc. All were headed for the bridge. By six o'clock, all groups had gone, and I alone was left in the lobby with the desk workers. If they wore uniforms or not, I didn't know. However, knowing even that bit of information would have been helpful when one Arabic-speaking man came and, in a heavy accent, said, "I'm Tony. I take you home and help you." I answered in Arabic, "No, thank you." There were two more men, each with different names, who again offered to take me to their homes. As eight o'clock drew near, I wondered if I had turned down the right designated man. How frightening! What if I had said "no" to the man who really was to help me!

After what seemed such a long time, the authorized man from the tour company came to take me to have new pictures made. Fortunately, I could at least greet him with a few phrases in Arabic. With the new pictures in hand, we rushed to the American Embassy; however, when we reached there to fill out papers for the new passport, we heard people making doubtful statements about being able to complete the process in time to get to the bridge before ten o'clock, especially since there was a waiting line. Yet, I saw no option but asking for that miracle. I prayed the Lord would give me favor so that the process could be hastened. In my heart I kept saying, "Lord, surround me with your favor as with a shield," as said in Psalm 5:12, "For thou, LORD, wilt bless the righteous; with favor wilt thou compass him as with a shield." I prayed, "Let us get to just the right worker, and let him have mercy and favor toward me." Some had said that it is possible that the authorized officials may not even be at their posts that day, because some people take vacation during Easter week. This was Wednesday before Easter, a holiday for some officials. God, however, who knew in advance of my arriving into that dilemma at that day, had placed the right people to expedite the processing of my new passport!

Speaking of holidays and sabbaths, it is important to understand the schedule of that particular week. First, Passover was going to be on Thursday, the day before what is traditionally called Good Friday. This meant that the Jewish customs officers on the Israeli side would close the bridge early on Wednesday. Israel's customs processing is very thorough; thus, anyone needing to cross from Jordan into Israel had to be on the bridge by ten in the morning in order for the Jewish officials to finish by noon, at which time they travel to their homes to prepare for the Passover. The Jewish new day begins at six in the evening, so Passover would start Wednesday at that time. This meant the Jewish side of the bridge would still be closed all day on Thursday.

The Muslim weekly sabbath is on Friday, thus the Jordanian (Arabic) side of the Allenby Bridge would be closed that day. The next day, Saturday, is the regular sabbath for the Jews, so the Jewish side would be closed again on that day. The next day would be Easter Sunday. Finding the guide in Israel or any officials on Easter would have been very difficult.

I had recommended a guide in Israel to Roger, but that guide had no phone. The tour group was to leave from Israel very early on Monday morning for Egypt. After two nights in Egypt, the group was to fly to Rome for a short tour, before flying back to New York. Here I was, however, separated from the group and stuck all alone in Ammon where I knew not even one person! I knew this schedule, so I realized that it was an absolute must that I meet up with my American group that very day, Wednesday.

As soon as the process was completed, I was given the new passport (and I asked for the old one back, which request they granted). To hasten processing of the new one, I told them that the cost is no issue, but just hurry. Again, fortunately, I knew how to say "hurry" and "thank you" in Arabic. As we all do, Arabs like to hear their own language, and it facilitates good rapport. Repeatedly, I said "Thank you."

The kind authorized helper put me into a cab and explained the situation to the driver, who, obviously understanding the need to hurry, nearly made the cab fly! He showed me the bar on the ceiling and told me to hang on tight. I asked his name. It was Pharez, and I asked him if he knew that his name was in the Bible. It is in the lineage of Jesus, Judah's son or Jacob's grandson. He was happy to hear that. Clearly, he was driving super fast, because I could feel the car's going around as it descended in altitude from Ammon down to the Allenby Bridge. I prayed for safety and held tightly. "Please, God, don't let us get a speeding ticket! That's all we need," I thought.

Finally, he said "We're here, and I think we got here in time, but I'm not sure." We jumped out of the cab and ran to the bridge. I could feel the whiz of the other buses returning eastward after delivering their tour groups to the customs officials. That bridge is quite narrow, leaving hardly any extra width, especially when a bus is rolling on it. My Jordanian cab driver could take me only to a certain point of the bridge, no farther. From that exact point, I'd need a helper from the

Jewish side to take me. As my helper and I were running on the bridge, I heard happy voices, yelling "Kim, Kim!" It was my own tour group that was waiting on the bridge to go through customs! Guess what time it was. It was exactly ten o'clock by now, so Pharez had put me on the bridge at 9:59, one minute before bridge closing time! My cab, I'm sure, was the last accepted vehicle for customs that day. The Lord had rescued me once again, just in the nick of time!

After writing the above paragraph, I e-mailed Roger, asking him how long the bus ride normally is from the hotel in Ammon to the Allenby Bridge. I knew it was more than one hour, but wasn't certain of the exact duration. Roger e-mailed back and said he believed two hours had been allotted for the bus trip. The more I think of God's helping me on that day, the greater the miracle becomes in my mind. In less than two hours, I had been picked up at the hotel, taken to a photo place, waited for the new passport photo to be developed, taken to the embassy, obtained the new passport, and rode (flew on ground) to the bridge! The Lord arranged all things, so that my speeding cab driver wasn't stopped for speeding! Surely He must have surrounded me with His favor and sent an angel before us at every point!

26. Tying Up Loose Ends

In writing this update to the original book, repeatedly I'm struck with the transitory nature of this life. One of the constantly occurring words in my mind is "ephemeral." So many people move away; others die, moving from here to eternity. How true that nothing on earth is secure! Another fact is that things don't wear up, or get better, with time; rather, things wear down, needing repair to be kept up or functional.

After I complete this writing project, repair of the Optacon awaits me. The OPtical to TActile CONverter has a panel of one hundred forty-four pinpoints that vibrate in the shape of each letter, so that the blind can slowly read regular print. I used that in Vienna for Bible reading. The same old model had served me until it required repair in 2004. That repair job didn't last long, as it has totally quit working. Although I don't use the Optacon daily, it is helpful for checking to see if I've addressed my outgoing mail correctly, and seeing from whom a piece of mail is.

The reason for checking my outgoing mail is because even when there is no more ink in the ribbon, the typewriter sounds the same. This happens also with my dot matrix printer; i.e., it makes the sound of printing, even if the ink has been depleted. Twice I've mailed a blank sheet of paper, not realizing that the ribbon was inkless. Thankfully, the friends phoned to alert me! One of them even took a pen, and by carefully tracing the slight indentations, he could outline each character, thus, figuring out the content of the entire page! What patience! Another time, the postman brought back a letter which I had sent out but which did not contain the address of the recipient because my typewriter ribbon had run out of ink. From that time on, I always write in Braille the name of the recipient on the outside of every outgoing envelope.

Truly, one of my prayers is, "Long as my life shall last, teach me Thy way." Even in the valleys or sad times, I ask Jesus, "What are You trying to teach me?" or "What am I to learn through this?" Much of the results of one's ministry won't be known until we all reach Heaven; however, occasionally, the Lord lets us have a sample of some of the results while we are still in this body. For example, some former prisoners have phoned me to say that they caught the first seed of the gospel through hearing me during their incarceration. When speaking in prisons, I often said that being blind is a form of a prison in which I've lived since age three. Jesus, however, helped me to leap over the walls of life's problems, turning the dark situations into light. He makes a way where there seems to be no way, humanly speaking. When He is invited into one's heart, He turns the night into day and gives him "The Song of the Soul Set Free." The ex-convicts have told me that they couldn't identify with the more famous Christians, but my speaking of being blind as a form of prison really "clicked" and got their attention.

Another good report was that at least two different mothers, whose children were blind, have told me that they figured God could make a way for their blind kids if God can take Kim around the world.

In singing for the military, I've enjoyed seeing the enthusiasm of soldiers, as they shout, "Air Assault!" They kept yelling that when I sang at Fort Campbell, and I couldn't even figure out what they were saying until one of them spelled the word "assault" to me! I've also held the limp hand of a dying soldier at a hospital, just a half hour before his death, telling him of Jesus. Since he had no strength left, he couldn't even talk. I don't know if he heard me, but someday in Heaven, I hope to see him.

At a 2001 concert in Baton Rouge, during the first part of the verbal testimony I mentioned how Hebrew as a language had been restored in Israel. Hearing Hebrew being spoken had helped me in reading the transliteration of Old Testament characters and places. Since I thought one of my friends from college days lived there, I tried to obtain his phone number from directory assistance, but to no avail. I thought perhaps he no longer was in the area, and I thought that I probably couldn't ever find out where he had relocated. After the concert, however, guess who was the first in line to greet me. It was that very friend whom the directory assistance had failed to find! We hadn't seen each other for thirty-three years, since 1968, when I was at Indiana University and he at Purdue. I told him that directory assistance could not find a listing for him. He told me that he was the chairman of the mathematics department at Louisiana State University and was en route from his office to home. Usually, he took a back way, but he thought, for a change, he'd take the main avenue. By so doing, he saw the "Kim Wickes in Concert" sign on the church, so in he came!

What is fascinating to me is that he is a Jew, and I had never before mentioned, in a concert, how the Jews have resurrected the Hebrew language for daily use. I stated that our English language changes so much, even just within decades, thus, what a miracle it was that the ancient Hebrew language has been restored for everyday use by all of Israel! At the time of sharing that early in the concert, I had no idea that this Jewish friend was in the audience, and it could well have been the first time of his attending an evangelical church. During the reception that followed, it was fun to hear of his successes, his family news, and of some of our mutual friends. Again, the Lord had providentially arranged the evening in a more efficient way than that of a human.

Through this concert ministry, the Lord has used me in greater degree than humans would have imagined, fulfilling His promise of Isaiah 42:16, "And I will bring the blind by a way that they knew not; I will lead them in paths that they have not known. . . ." This was the life verse given me as a ten-year-old, in 1957, by the missionary as I left Korea to be adopted. There have been six return trips to Korea. One was with the Billy Graham team to celebrate the centennial of the first missionaries reaching Korea with the gospel. On one of the solo mission trips to Korea, it was a thrill to be able to raise sufficient funds to help a blind men's quartet to buy a van so they could travel to start their singing ministry. This was done via ticket sales for my concert at Sejong Cultural Center in Seoul. The president of South Korea and his wife attended. (Billy Kim did the scheduling for most of my mission trips.) Also on that particular trip, enough finances came in for us to provide coats for old folks in a retirement home. But most of all, so many people accepted Jesus on these trips!

Mission trips took me to the French-speaking island of Guadaloupe, West Indies, as well as back to the Philippines. During one visit, I challenged the audience in the Philippine International Convention Center to give financially in order to help a province that had suffered famine due to the sugarcane crop failure that year. Of course, that trip included the usual concerts, TV and radio appearances, and school chapel services, in addition to the fundraising evening. I mention the convention center meeting in particular because the appeal had to be given in the native tongue, Tagaloc. No, I don't speak Tagaloc, but memorized only pertinent sentences by rote to inspire the audience to give. You may recall that I was teased as a little girl in the orphanage in Korea when teachers and kids called me a pig and/or a monkey. That used to make me feel somewhat bad. However, in 1974 the teacher of that orphanage told me the reason for having been called such things. She said it was because I could copy anything. That ability facilitates language learning. Apparently, the decision-makers in the mission trip to the Philippines assigned me to the task of speaking Tagaloc for a good purpose. It was just for that one event, and only the necessary sentences were taught me. God's work was furthered, however, by my ability to listen and imitate.

Another facet of my ministry was singing for various prayer groups of senators and congressmen in Washington, D.C., with former Senator Jesse Helms of North Carolina being the one with whom I had the most association. For example, at a dinner for his announcing his first re-election, I sang several church songs and gave my personal testimony. That evening sounded more like a revival service than a political event.

In 1984, while I was singing in the D.C. area, Senator Helms held a private reception in his office for his staff and me. When I think of the myriad of responsibilities of such a senator, I'm humbled and honored at his taking time for little me. It is no less than God fulfilling Proverbs 18:16: "A man's gift maketh room for him, and bringeth him before great men." Thank God for the gift of music and for kind men who made time in their busy schedules for me! There were other times of singing for him, too. The last was in July 1997, when he was honored for twenty-five years of serving as a senator. That program was later telecast on C-Span. One of the proud watchers of that telecast was the mother of one of my Wheaton Academy classmates.

That classmate is Ginger Johnson, mentioned in my original book. Her mother characteristically redressed an injustice with justice, i.e., turned a wrong into a right. In 1981, after one of my concerts at Wheaton, Ginger's mother surprised me by having the Wheaton Academy headmaster present me with a National Honor Society pin.

She thought that mistake of the past should be rectified. You may recall that I was not inducted into the honor society during high school in 1965. That situation didn't seem fair to my friends or to me. Later that same year of 1981, I gave a concert at Wheaton Academy during homecoming weekend. At the end of that concert, I was honored with the outstanding alumnae award. Subsequently, many other members from my class have received that award. In fact, I even suggested some of those recipients.

In thinking over the years subsequent to the first publishing of this book, I can't help but realize how ephemeral earthly things are. The brevity of this whole earthly life really hits home when I remember having sung for Ginger's wedding in 1968, then for her dad's funeral in 1976, and then for her mother's funeral in 2000.

Since in Hebrews 12:1 this life is compared to running a race, I visualize it as a race in which each one of us is running in his assigned lane and at a pace and manner unique only to that individual, who is unlike any other person ever created in all of human history. It is reported that there are no two snowflakes exactly alike; likewise, I'm certain there is never a duplicate of you or me, for God never runs out of new patterns. Everyone He sends to this planet has his own blueprint. I can't do what someone else is to do; conversely, nobody else can quite do what I'm supposed to do.

This principle applies to the fact that I felt led, early in my ministry, to do what is called traditional music; e.g., mostly heartfelt hymns, a few classical numbers, and even fewer contemporary songs, even though it may have meant selling fewer recordings. I felt I had to stay in the lane assigned to me by the Lord. He had prepared me through years of training and even borrowed funds. (Incidentally, I didn't even buy a new suitcase until my student loans had all been paid . . . and before interest kicked in. The Lord showed me this was prudent.) Even the little children and youths listen to my music and testimony attentively, and I'm sure it is the Holy Spirit who demonstrates to them the reality of what is being sung or verbally shared. Many say that my music isn't an entertainment, but as Dr. James Kennedy says, "It is a benediction." Proverbs 22:28 says, "Remove not the ancient landmark, which thy fathers have set." This command is re-emphasized by Proverbs 23:10: "Remove not the old landmark." Perhaps I'm crazy, but my *modus operandi* is to find something that works and stick with it, and my ministering via traditional music is no exception to this philosophy.

Although my basic preference of music style hasn't altered, the pace of travel changes as I experience various seasons of ministry. For example, for more than twenty years I almost lived on airplanes, sometimes two or three in one day. However, now I perform locally or within a day's driving distance.

As I meditate on how the Lord has led different people to be in this locale at this time, it is neat to see His sovereign schedule in their lives. In May 1994, Pastor Yoong Kim began a Korean church in Memphis. I regularly sing and teach flute there. In June of 1995, David Moose came to Rosewood Methodist Church in West Memphis as both the pastor and the choir director. Having been in Lions Club for forty years, Brother David has a special spot in his heart for the blind. During the last twenty years he has had personal battles with visual disorders. Pastor Kim, who first came to my concert in Memphis in January 1975, also understands the blind well. His wife became legally blind in 1994, necessitating, the sale of her business which she had owned for nineteen years. Vision of 20/200 is considered legally blind. Both pastors sing well.

At this point, a discussion of various degrees of blindness may be illuminative. Many people say that I see "pitch black" or "darkness" all the time; however, this is incorrect. It takes sight to see even darkness or pitch blackness. I recall seeing during the first three years of life, and having experienced sight even that short period is something for which I'm grateful. Obviously, those of us with two prosthetic eyes are what is called "totally blind." Sight is nonexistent or, as I say, just "zero." I am unable to distinguish the difference between a light being on or off.

Then there is a greater number of people who are "legally blind." They can see partially, seeing light, colors, presence of objects and persons, etc. However, such person's sight is insufficient for driving a car. Pastor Kim's wife reached this point. While her vision is lacking for her reading regular print, some legally blind people can read by using magnifying instruments, even if they can't see enough to drive.

In this modern age of so much computerization, I see the frustration resulting from political correctness, where the word "blind" is avoided and the phrase "visually impaired" or "visually challenged" replaces it. Let me illustrate. Even with my phoning every month to explain my being totally (not just partially) blind, literally for years, my credit card bill kept coming to me in "large print" instead of in Braille. By that I deduced that the only "field" or "code" which had been programmed in the bank's software was "visual impairment" or something to that affect. I couldn't read the statement if every character were three inches tall! Oh, I could tell of many such experiences, but suffice it to say, this political correctness seems unnecessary and inadequate, because it avoids telling the truth about a situation. To me, it is just being honest to say, "I'm blind."

Finally, in stating that Pastor Moose battles his own sight disorders, I should clarify that he can read, drive, and see the computer screen adequately. Just for the sake of information, I'd like to say that a relatively small percentage of the blind uses Braille; i.e., there are more blind people who do not use it than there are who do, particularly in this modern age of talking computers, talking microwaves, talking watches, etc. Personally, I prefer Braille whenever possible, because I think a talking watch might be disruptive in a meeting.

About leading the blind, I say to the leader, "Do like Jesus and set the example by going a step ahead of me, and give me room to copy you. The best way is to let me put my hand at the crux of your arm." Allowing space for the blind to copy is important, as when navigating steps or a doorway. Don't put the blind in front of you and push him like a cart ahead of you. That isn't how Jesus leads. The key is to set the example. By this principle, people all over the globe have helped me, even if they had not ever walked with the blind previously.

My singing in the Korean church choir is another example of a miracle that should be explained. The choir began singing regularly in late 1999 when the Korean language still sounded quite foreign to me. Remember, I had concentrated on learning Western languages, including English, German, French, and Italian. I hadn't done anything in Korean Braille since 1957. With learning each language, the Braille system of that language must also be learned. Braille is a system of dots, but the meaning of each dot combination varies according to the language. Miraculously, when I wanted to write the words to the choir hymn, all the contractions and every character's dot combination came back to me. This means the Lord resurrected my knowledge of Korean Braille after forty-two years! In the interim, I had even seen Braille in Arabic, along with the above mentioned European languages. While someone dictates the text to the choir song on the phone, I write it all in Braille on thick paper. Braille dots naturally last longer on the thicker paper than they would on regular thin paper. This paper can be purchased in individual sheets with three holes already punched. However, it is more expensive, so I buy computer fanfold paper as needed. Periodically, I must punch holes for my three-ring binder and separate them into individual sheets.

Any song, once put into Braille, is kept in a wire clasp so that repeating the work won't be necessary for the next use of that song.

During time-consuming tasks, such as punching holes in paper and separating individual pages, I tell myself, ". . . whatsoever ye do, do all to the glory of God" (1 Cor. 10:31). Someone's dictating the Korean text helps me, so that in turn I can help the choir; thus, once again, an example of how the body of Christ functions. In other words, every member of the body of Jesus has an important purpose. No one can do or know everything; however, each one of us can do and know something. Let's faithfully operate in our assigned slot!

In trying to tie up some loose ends, I'll share that I wrote a letter of gratitude to the Bible teacher and phoned the choir director of my junior year at Wheaton Academy, expressing my appreciation for all they had taught me. Also, to my adopted parents I wrote more than once to express my genuine thanks for their bringing me to the United States. Moreover, a couple of the faculty members from Indiana University days have received letters from me, too. I wanted them to know how much they meant to me, and how much I enjoyed seeing them again. It was encouraging when an Indiana University voice teacher wrote me a complimentary letter after seeing me on "The Hour of Power" telecast from Garden Grove, California.

Speaking of university days, I even searched out the phone number of a college contemporary who was not even in the School of Music. I apologized for not knowing how to show more compassion when his relative had died with cancer when we were both in graduate school and in the same dorm. Actually, back then, I hadn't even heard of a sympathy card; thus, all I had mumbled was, "I'm sorry. That's bad." I didn't want this life to pass without my having communicated to all the people above.

John Humes passed away before I had an opportunity of expressing my gratitude. Mr. Humes was the United States ambassador to Austria while I was a Fulbright student in Vienna. It had been his idea that I go see my biological father in Korea, en route back to

America, at the end of the Fulbright year. He felt so strongly about this that he even paid the additional cost of that ticket in 1974. As the years passed, I had no idea how to locate Mr. Humes. However, twenty-four years after his act of kindness, God led me to someone who did know. On a flight from Atlanta to Fort Myers, Florida, in February 1998, I was sharing my testimony with the man in the next seat. When I mentioned the generous ambassador who had helped with the ticket back to Korea, my seat partner asked, "That wouldn't be John Humes, would it?" I exclaimed, "Yes! Do you know how I could contact him?" He said that John Humes was deceased, but his widow would love to hear from me. The passenger right then and there gave me her address. I wrote her immediately after returning home. Upon receiving my letter, she kindly replied, thanking me, and stated that her late husband would have appreciated my letter. I wish I'd learned the contact information earlier so that he could have read it before his passing. When it comes to encouraging and thanking another pilgrim as we travel on this journey called life, "better late than never" really is true.

At one point in composing this life's story, I had thought of mentioning the names of other dear ones who have died. In an effort to prevent this from becoming an obituary column, that idea has been abandoned. Instead, I will summarize two of the messages I vividly recall from my junior year Bible class at Wheaton Academy. That was actually my first year there, because I had spent the previous two high school years at Indiana School for the Blind. The first of these lectures is that "conflicts are inevitable" in life. Wow! How true that has proven to be! The second message was how we should take advantage of every opportunity to witness for the Lord, while we can. Early in life, opportunities are EVERYWHERE. As time passes, we realize opportunities are ebbing. Soon, we reach the point where opportunities are ended! As our English teacher of that same year used to say, "A word to the wise is sufficient."

Since people sometimes ask if I've ever been in a scary situation, I'll now cite some examples of dangers from which God has delivered me. There are more than a few, but I'll mention just two. Once in a home where I was spending Saturday night before a Sunday morning concert, there was a physically large eleven-year-old boy with Down's Syndrome. He couldn't speak a word. As usual, Murphy's Law was in motion. Even though their air conditioner was broken on that hot August night in Georgia, I was still determined to do sit-up exercises before washing and rolling my hair on "umpteen" curlers. In order to make enough floor space available for doing sit-ups, the boy's older sister moved a chair in the living room. She then went to another part of the house. What was unknown to me was that the slightest rearrangement of even one chair would upset the Down's Syndrome boy. As I lay on my back to start the sit-ups, I felt something swinging from side to side above my forehead, not actually hitting me but close enough that I could feel its movement and hear the slight swish-h-h of each swing. I could also hear the boy breathing heavily, and I could sense that he was displeased about something. When I called for his sister, she came running and saw that he was swinging a golf club over my forehead! After moving him to a different room and closing the door, she explained that he gets upset if an object is moved even the slightest distance from its normal location. In the middle of that night, I was suddenly awakened by his running into his bed, in which I was sleeping. By then, I could understand what was happening. Not only had he seen new objects, such as my cosmetic bag in the bathroom, but had also given up his bedroom for me! The earlier episode of his golf club swinging had enlightened me to realize that any change was upsetting to him.

A second scary episode occurred right here in my home office, on August 1, 2006, when I sat down directly on a wasp who was lying in ambush on the chair in front of the computer. When I sat down I knew something had bitten me, and I automatically let out a scream. Fortunately, I had a Kleenex in my pocket. I wrapped the tissue around the culprit on my chair, praying that the thing wouldn't hurt my fingers. I squeezed it millimeter by millimeter, until I had squeezed the whole length of him. I then limped to a phone to call Joy Sample, saying, "Something has bitten me; I need help." She was baking cookies for a funeral but said she'd come when she reached a stopping point. When she came and looked in the Kleenex, she told me it was a wasp. To make a long story short, we did what we could, including phoning my doctor. By the next morning, I could see that the skin was swelling with infection. Upon calling the doctor for an appointment, I was told no slot was available until the following afternoon. Even though I was applying ice, it continued to swell. My friends said I should have insisted it was an emergency, but I was too reluctant to be that assertive for myself. (For someone else, I could have been assertive!) Finally, when the doctor saw me after two days, he said, "UGLY infection!" Ridding that infection took more than a month of oral antibiotics and antihistamines, but I still went to church every Sunday. I used a water bottle, filled with ice, and sat on it all day long, in the car and during the church service.

With assurance of God's deliverance, Job 5:22 says, "At destruction and famine thou shalt laugh: neither shalt thou be afraid of the beasts of the earth." Part of my regular prayer is that God will deliver me from every critter and insect, asking His angels around me to keep them away from me. Incidentally, that wasp left his mark on my seat, a small bump like a big Braille dot, but under the skin where he deposited his stinger. (The wondrous facet of this episode is that it did pass. The last time I was stung was at the university. The doctor said that one more sting would kill me . . . but, I'm not dead yet!)

Since the Bible says for us to muse and meditate on what God has done for us, writing this update has afforded a fitting opportunity to reflect on my life and how far God has brought me. For example, as I've frequently said, I started my life with not even one bathroom, and now I have to clean multiple toilets! Having them to clean is infinitely better than not having one. Also, I began life with starvation, but now I have to schedule when to diet! Every time I peel a boiled egg, I think of the early years of my life. I used to hunt in people's garbage for even just one piece of the membrane of an egg shell to eat. Nowadays, as I discard the entire membrane with the whole egg shell, I gratefully exclaim, "Lord, look how far You've brought me!" Psalm 126:3 describes it aptly, "The LORD hath done great things for us; whereof we are glad." Furthermore, a dirt floor or outside ground was my bed in the early years. Now what a blessing is a really good, modern bed! Every night I praise the Lord, saying, "Thank you for this home and everything therein: Thy word, this bed, piano, computers, for I know every good and perfect gift comes from Thee!"

All my friends thrill at going through this home, calling it a mini-museum. One item which I always enjoy showing is the Braille Bible. My Bible takes up sixty inches of book shelf space! Since Braille requires so much paper, even with using contractions, one Bible consists of eighteen large volumes. Obviously, each volume must always be returned to its proper place.

Since underlining or highlighting in the Braille Bible isn't possible, and because I love God's words, I try diligently to memorize as much as possible, particularly passages applicable to current circumstances; i.e., those that "hit the spot!" The things of earth truly do become unimportant as we realize how vitally important the Bible is. Some call me a "Walking Bible" or "Kimchi Concordance." To me, these are real compliments. That name, which came from the "Kimchi Computer," was started by some college friends and has continued among my Korean friends. However, I always assure them that it fits only in reference to the subject matter of the Bible (through which I try to read yearly), not to worldly matters.

In reflecting on the Lord's work in my life, I can't help but thank Him for letting me be in school at the right time, as well as for having me fly so much when He did. Flying has become more complicated after September 11, 2001. Also, during my college years, there were numerous times that I walked alone after midnight more than a mile from the music school to the graduate dorm. Nowadays, it would be unthinkable to walk alone with a cane, as even a sighted person is encouraged to move around on campus in a crowd rather than alone. The sovereign God certainly did order my steps aright! In my days of walking alone at night, my only prayer was, "Lord, please don't let a UFO get me!" Would that such were our only problem today!

I'd like to mention here three frequent sayings from my heart. First, "Life is one continuous juggling act; balancing can only be maintained by the Lord Himself." About the time we think that the ducks are in a row, inevitably some ducks fall out of line! That's why the Bible says four times that the just shall live by faith. Second, "Think or sink." This is a motto which the Lord gave me very early in my ministry. I have had it framed, and that frame hangs in my office. Third, Mary Crowley, founder of Home Interiors and Gifts, taught us the ten two-letter words that make history: "If it is to be, it is up to me." I've continually reminded myself of these ten words in trying to write this update.

As the years go by, our surroundings change. Many people move away or die. I pray the Lord will continue sending other right people. All of you who have heard my concerts know that I always credit God for helping me not to be afraid when my biological father threw me into the river to drown. In this He was fulfilling His promise of Isaiah 43:1–2: ". . . Fear not: for I have redeemed thee, I have called thee by thy name; thou art mine. When thou passest through the waters, I will be with thee; and through the rivers, they shall not overflow thee."

After turning fifty years of age, I see so many dear ones dying. My friend, Margaret, jokingly says, "You're going to live to one hundred and fifty in a nursing home, but all your friends will be dead." I have to stand firmly on Isaiah 43:4: "Since thou wast precious in my sight, thou hast been honorable, and I have loved thee: therefore will I give men for thee, and people for thy life." (She proudly wears a vest that I designed and knitted for her.) My answer to her is always that I pray for the Rapture, so that we can all go together. If we have to go by death instead, all I can do is trust Him, knowing that my times are in His hand (Ps. 31:15). Incidentally, if the Lord tarries and I have to go by physical death, I'm a body donor, as I don't see the need of paying for a plot of dirt for this tent of dust to occupy! Others can be helped by organ donations, as well as by medical research performed on a donated body. Even in death I want to help others.

For decades, I've spoken and sung about Jesus's second coming, realizing that there won't be peace on earth, and certainly not in Jerusalem, until the Prince of Peace actually returns to earth. Of receiving at least one crown in Heaven, I'm quite sure, and that would be the crown of righteousness, not because of being "holier than thou," but because of loving His appearing, as we read in 2 Timothy 4:8: "Henceforth there is laid up for me a crown of righteousness, which the Lord, the righteous judge, shall give me at that day: and not to me only, but unto all them also that love his appearing." I truly do long to see Him. Besides, by so many having been promoted via death already, there are more friends up in Heaven than there are left here on earth.

Even some of my Christian friends say to me that things have been as they are now for thousands of years and it will continue being that way for thousands of more years. My reply to them is that they are unknowingly but exactly fulfilling the prophecy found in 2

Peter 3:3–4: "Knowing this first, that there shall come in the last days scoffers, walking after their own lusts, saying, Where is the promise of his coming? for since the fathers fell asleep, all things continue as they were from the beginning of the creation." Others say that the world has always been sinful, but modern technology just enables all nations to see it simultaneously. In my way of thinking, however, the media has led people to be proud of wrong doing, rather than being ashamed. Just as in Jeremiah's time, humans don't know how to blush, or be ashamed, at committing sin. I truly do believe iniquity is waxing ever stronger. Why? It is because the evil one, Lucifer, also knows that his time is short.

On September 11, 2001, we witnessed the incredibly wicked works of Satan, as his deception manifested itself through the Islamic *jihadists*. From then on, daily I speak with the Lord, quoting Revelation 3:10: "Because thou hast kept the word of my patience, I also will keep thee from the hour of temptation, which shall come upon all the world, to try them that dwell upon the earth." Then I say to Jesus, "Lord, hasn't it already come upon ALL the world?" It surely looks like it to me. As the terrorists gird the entire globe with such deep-seated intrinsic hatred, but are so convinced of being in the right, I don't see how Jesus's return could be not imminent. He alone can straighten out everything.

Of all the horrors of September 11, 2001, the brave passengers of United Flight 93, along with all the firemen and the police who courageously charged into the inferno, are my real heroes. Anyone who has been around me has heard my frequent use of the following: The greatest privilege in life is to be a citizen of Heaven by having invited Jesus into my heart, and the second greatest privilege is to be the citizen of the best nation on the planet, the United States. Both of these privileges are made possible because of adoption. We are spiritually adopted into God's family by placing our trust in Jesus.

Through reading letters (from Wheaton Academy), I learned of Todd Beamer's affiliation with Wheaton Academy and Wheaton College. "What could I personally do?" I thought. I wrote to Lisa Beamer, his young widow, and offered to give a benefit concert, with the proceeds applied toward any purpose of her choosing and that I'd pay for my own plane ticket for the event. Feeling so helpless, I thought this was the least I could do. Since she was involved with so many new developments at the time in October 2001, I didn't receive a direct response. However, after she founded the organization called Heroic Choices, I began receiving its informational correspondence. As the Lord enables me, I give some financially to this valuable work, as its leaders strive to continue Todd's ministry to the youth.

Furthermore, although I usually don't go to movies, I strongly believed that every American ought to see *United 93,* and it was good to find friends who were kind enough to take me. I go to so few movies that the number I've attended could be literally counted on my fingers . . . and have fingers left over. I deeply appreciate the passengers of Flight 93 and heartily applaud the continuing positive efforts of the surviving families. "Lead on, Lisa, and God bless you at every step!"

In connection with the war on terror, I saw the hand of God in leading me to sing exactly the right solo on Sunday, October 7, 2001. I sang "If God Be for Us, Who Can Be Against Us" from *The Messiah.* That solo happened at eleven thirty in the morning, Central Time, but I didn't hear until that evening about our military's going into Afghanistan at that very hour during my solo. I thought, "How providentially chosen was that song!"

As I've stated earlier, I ask the Lord to teach me His way, even when something bad happens in life. I've observed that every culture and every denomination can offer something positive which we can learn. Conversely, every group also has negative facets which we must discard. I pray for the Lord to help me to glean the good and dump the bad from each ethnic group and denomination. I guess one thing which we can learn from the *jihadists* is commitment. If we Christians were as dedicated to Jesus as they are to the wrong, how much more could be accomplished for the Lord!

While writing this update, I've realized the reason for some of my physical features. These features brought hurtful comments earlier in my life, but God had a purpose for everything. Namely, my head is too fat and my diaphragm sticks out. Both are equipment for God's plan for me. Breathing deeply is essential for correct singing and public speaking, so the diaphragm naturally develops. Also, about being teased as a "fat head," I now say "Ah, so" because a light bulb has come on. In addition to the echo chamber for singing, some space was necessary for a little bit of brains, too! In fact, a retired math teacher told me that I was one of the two brightest students in all her career. Friends who know me well have also said, "You're the smartest woman I've ever met." Of course, I know mental ability is a God-given survival kit of tools, not anything for which I can take credit!

When I'm in need of physical or emotional healing, I sing the music of Mozart, my favorite composer. My most frequent choice is "Alleluja" from *Exsultate, Jubilate*. I think his is the closest to Heaven's music.

As for hymns, when comfort is needed, I sing "It Is Well with My Soul" and "Teach Me Thy Way." The most requested song by others is "The Lord's Prayer," self-accompanied on piano. Many have said that nobody anywhere does it better. For that I thank the Lord for His anointing.

When I see the inextricably entangled web of today's world, I say that there are two women whom I'll whip when I get to Heaven: Eve and Sarah. My words will be, "Did you have to?"

Seriously, I'm sure we'll be so thrilled at the quick metamorphosis into immortality that I'll forget the above thought! Until then, I joy in Isaiah 56:4–5: "For thus saith the LORD unto the eunuchs that keep my sabbaths, and choose the things that please me, and take hold of my covenant; Even unto them will I give in mine house and within my walls a place and a name better than of sons and of daughters: I will give them an everlasting name, that shall not be cut off." After Dr. Carl Baugh, founder and director of Creation Evidence Museum (in Glen Rose, Texas), had read my life story, he phoned to encourage me, stating that the Lord will make up to me a thousand times for anything that I've missed down here.

Some rewards have already come. Being nominated as an outstanding woman of America is an example. Also after my singing at his crusades, Mr. Graham said I sang the gospel as few on earth have done. (I was saved at the Graham crusade held in Indianapolis in 1959. In 1980, I returned to that city to sing in the Graham crusade.) Furthermore, Pastor Kim has said that the best part of coming to church is to hear Kim sing. Numerous others around the world have said that they see Jesus in my life, commenting on how my music must be like that of Heaven. These are beginnings of God's making up for some of the good things I've missed. Incidentally, people sometimes say, "I'd give everything to sing like you." My reply, "I did." By that I mean, everything in life is a trade-off; i.e., we give up one thing in order to gain another, since each of us has just twenty-four hours in a day.

Because God has promised to give the right people into my life, I claim Psalm 142:7: ". . . the righteous shall compass me about; for thou shalt deal bountifully with me." I pray the Lord surrounds me with the righteous and shields me from the wrong ones, realizing that each changing future scene must be entrusted to Him.

As new friends come into my life, they enjoy seeing my house. In directing them to visit me, one feature always mentioned is the American flag in the driveway. All enjoy seeing my home, watching me work in the office, seeing my reading to them from the Braille

Bible, playing the piano and singing for them, and then in learning that I do all the house cleaning myself. We praise the Lord together for His enabling all this, as I remind everyone that every good gift comes from Him, and we are mere stewards. In other words, God is the landlord, and we are the tenants.

Singing and piano playing are done in the front part of the house. When I sing, a fun thing is that the birds also sing from right outside the front door, sitting either in the bushes or on the iron fence that supports the mailbox. Later in the day, when I play the flute from the back part of the house, the den, the birds sing just outside the den door, too. In fact, they have built nests in the gutter immediately outside the den/kitchen area. Around here, it is far preferable that there be nests of birds than of wasps since I'm so allergic to stings!

During these last few weeks of concentrating exclusively on writing this update, housekeeping, music, and even exercising have been on hold; therefore, cares of this life will require much attention after the completion of this project.

Another part of my daily prayers is 1 Thessalonians 5:23–24: "And the very God of peace sanctify you [me] wholly; and I pray God your whole spirit and soul and body be preserved blameless unto the coming of our Lord Jesus Christ. Faithful is he that calleth you, who also will do it." If it weren't for this last verse, I'd not have attempted writing this update!

Perchance you, my reader friend, may not yet have made sure of Heaven being your eternal home. For many years, I've known that Christians go to Heaven, but I didn't put it all together that the unbeliever will actually be somewhere forever too; i.e., in a lake of fire, where the fire never goes out, and the worm never dies. If you aren't sure that you will go to Heaven, please pray the following:

Lord Jesus Christ, I'm a sinner, but I want to be yours as of this moment. I repent of my sins. Please forgive them all, and count me as one of yours. Wash me with your blood and cleanse me. Come into my heart right now. I do believe you are the only Saviour, and that for me you died on the cross and rose from the dead. Thank you for saving me into your family. I pray in Your holy name. Amen

In tying up loose ends, I might mention another frequently asked question, which is, "How do you get your news?" and my answer is primarily by listening to Paul Harvey, my favorite reporter and commentator. On more than one occasion he has mentioned my story on the air, something which I consider an honor. He writes of how audiences are mesmerized and brought to their feet all over the world by my concerts. In addition, he shares Billy Graham's statement, made after my solo at his twenty-fifth anniversary crusade in the Hollywood Bowl, "Some of the best music that the Hollywood Bowl has ever heard."

Through the years, "Father Graham" has given me such compliments for a brochure and also has used my life as an example of God's grace in some of his own books. Dr. Harvey continues in his article, stating that I have entertained and motivated uncounted millions on every continent. His high assessment is, of course, humbling to me because he adds, "We, who have heard her in person, have heard vocal music with the delicacy of a bird song, and with the mighty and majestic heavenly host of angels." How aptly his final description summarizes my heart's earnest desire for this ministry! "It is the music of the night, which is now turning the light on all over the world!"

As I've tried to shed the light of Jesus into this dark world, it is interesting to realize that the first foreign language into which the original publication of my story was translated was French in Switzerland. One might have expected Korean, but that was the second language into which it was translated. As for the movie that wasn't made, at least not at this writing, Ike Smith says that it is just as well, because, "So many wouldn't believe it, as truth is more unbelievable than fiction." Indeed, there have been those who told me to quit making up tales when they hear my testimony. As long as the Lord enables, each of us must do his best, in his assigned niche, and in a manner unique only to him.

Finally, Hebrews 13:16 says: "But to do good and to communicate forget not: for with such sacrifices God is well pleased." I have tried to communicate by writing this addition to my life story. To each of you who has trusted Jesus as Saviour, let me thank you for reading this. I'll surely see you, if not here, in the air, or up there, and soon, because I believe Jesus' return is imminent! I pray several times daily, "Even so, Lord Jesus, please come quickly!" Amen.

Kim Wickes was born in Korea. After being blinded by a bomb during the Korean War, she was adopted by an American family. Kim earned a Masters in music from Indiana University. Subsequently, she graduated from the Vienna Institute of Music on a Fulbright scholarship. Kim speaks four languages, and she has sung at Billy Graham Crusades, international Christian conventions, and churches around the world. She is known as one of the finest Christians vocalists of our time.

ISBN 1-933641-17-7
Music CD   Approximately 1½ hours
Retail — $12.95

Ring the Bells
Angels We Have Heard on High
Go Tell It On the Mountain
Silent Night
Some Children See Him
Down From His Glory
Sweet Little Jesus Boy
O Holy Night
There Is a Balm in Gilead
My Heavenly Father Watches Over Me
Thanks Be to God
Praise the Lord
Amazing Grace
The Lord Is My Light
The Lord's Prayer
God Bless America
The Holy City
Without Him
His Eye Is on the Sparrow
Song of the Soul Set Free
How Great Thou Art
Thank You, God, for Jesus
I Walked Today Where Jesus Walked
No One Ever Cared for Me Like Jesus
Jesus Is Coming Again